Kindle Fire HDX User Manual

The Ultimate Guide for Mastering Your Kindle HDX

Owner of the new Kindle Fire HDX?

Learn what most owners of this new tablet DON'T...and transform this powerful device into your ultimate entertainment and productivity machine!

By
Daniel Forrester
Author & Tech Enthusiast

Table of Contents

What's In The Box?

Your Kindle Fire HDX box should contain:

Kindle Fire HDX (1)
Either the 7-inch model or the 8.9-inch model

USB Cable (1)
This cable will be used to charge your device (by connecting it with the power adapter) as well as transfer files from your PC/Mac to your Kindle Fire HDX (and vice-versa).

Power Adapter (1)
This connects to your USB cable to form a charger, which can be plugged into an outlet.

Quick Start Guide (1)
This is a small sheet that contains quick-start instruction for your Kindle Fire HDX.

Kindle Fire HDX Specifications

	Kindle Fire HD	Kindle Fire HD 8.9	Kindle Fire HDX	Kindle Fire HDX 8.9
Cost	Starts at $139	Starts at $229	Stars at $229	Stars at $379
Screen	7-inch	8.9-inch	7-inch	8.9-inch
Screen Resolution	1280x800 (216 ppi)	1920x1200 (254 ppi)	1920x1200 (323 ppi)	2560x1600 (339 ppi)
Processor	1.5 GHz Dual Core	1.5 GHz Dual Core	2.2 GHz Quad Core	2.2 GHz Quad Core
Battery	10 hours	10 hours	11 hrs / 17 hrs while reading	12 hrs / 18 hrs while reading
Audio	Dolby, Dual Stereo Speakers	Dolby, Dual Stereo Speakers, Built-in Mic	Dolby, Dual Stereo Speakers, Built-in Mic	Dolby, Dual Stereo Speakers, Built-in Mic
Wi-Fi	Dual band	Dual band & Dual antenna	Dual band & Dual antenna	Dual band & Dual antenna
4G Capability	None	Yes	Yes	Yes
Camera	No Camera	Front-facing (HD)	Front-facing (HD)	Front-facing (HD) & Rear-facing (8MP)
Hard Drive	8GB or 16GB	16GB, 32GB or 64GB (only on 4G)	16GB, 32GB or 64GB	16GB, 32GB or 64GB
Weight	12.2oz	20oz	Wi-Fi: 10.7oz, 4G: 11oz	Wi-Fi: 13.2oz, 4G: 13.5oz
Support	Email, Phone, Web	Email, Phone, Web	"MayDay" button, email, phone + web	"MayDay" button, email, phone + web
Software	Fire OS 3.0 "Mojito"	Kindle Fire OS 2.0	Fire OS 3.0 "Mojito"	Fire OS 3.0 "Mojito"

Kindle Fire HDX 7" Specifications

The Kindle Fire HDX comes in two different screen sizes: the 7-inch and 8.9-inch. The 7-inch model comes equipped with one of the three different storage sizes: 16GB, 32GB, and 64GB.

There is also an option to select whether your device will come equipped with or without "Special Offers". Selecting the "Special Offers" option will cause your device to display ads on the lock screen (like a screensaver), but reduces the purchase price. You can pay an additional fee to remove special offers after purchasing your device, so it does not matter which option you've selected for your HDX.

There are several different options for Internet connectivity. You can select Wi-Fi Only, or if you would like Internet connectivity anywhere you go, you can select WiFi + 4G for AT&T or Verizon, depending on your preferred carrier. You will have to contact your mobile carrier to select the data plan you wish to connect your HDX to.

The Kindle Fire HDX 7-inch has a 1920x1200 screen, with a high pixel density (323 PPI) as well as perfect color accuracy (100% sRGB) for unmatched image representation and video playback. The processor is the most powerful for a 7-inch tablet: a 2.2GHz quad-core processor as well as 2GB of RAM, which allows for seamless video and smooth gaming. All Kindle Fire HDX's come loaded with Amazon's new operating system, the Fire OS 3.0 or "Mojito".

The Kindle Fire HDX 7-inch provides extended battery life; about 11 hours of heavy usage per charge and about 17 hours when you are just using your device for just reading.

Kindle Fire HDX 8.9" Specifications

Like the HDX 7-inch, the 8.9-inch comes in 3 different hard drive sizes: 16GB, 32GB, and 64GB. You can also select with or without "Special Offers", as well as Wi-Fi Only or Wi-Fi with a 4G+ data plan utilizing either AT&T or Verizon's service.

The HDX 8.9-inch boasts a 2560x1600 screen, with a pixel density of 339PPI and a color accuracy of 100% sRGB for beautiful image viewing and crisp HD video. The device weighs in at 13.2oz (34% less heavy than the previous HD model) and is ultra thin. The HDX 8.9-inch contains a 2.2GHz quad-core processor – which is three times more powerful than the previous Kindle's. It also comes stocked with 2GB of RAM and an

Adreno 330 GPU, which allows for a high-powered video and gaming experience (4 times the speed of the previous Kindle model).

The HDX 8.9-inch differs from the 7-inch model as it comes with an 8 mega-pixel rear-facing camera that includes LED flash and 1080p HD video support. Both the Kindle Fire HDX 7-inch and 8.9-inch come with the front facing 720p HD Camera, which is great for Skype and video calls.

The Kindle Fire HDX 8.9 also provides extended battery life (slightly longer battery life than the 7" model). The battery provides for about 12 hours of heavy usage per charge and about 18 hours when just using it for reading.

Kindle Fire HDX vs. Kindle Fire HD

Both the Kindle Fire HD and HDX come in two different sizes: 7-inch and 8.9-inch. The HDX offers a 1920 x 1200 pixel screen (323ppi) for the 7-inch model and 2560 x 1600 pixel resolution (339ppi) for the 8.9-inch. This makes the Kindle Fire HDX the tablet with the sharpest display in the world.

The latest Kindle Fire HD (7-inch) boasts a 1280 x 800 screen (with 216ppi). The Kindle Fire HD 8.9-inch offers a 1920 x 1200 display (254ppi). Thus, the HDX has a sharper resolution, as the pixel density is greater.

Both HDX models contain a 2.2GHz processor (quad-core, dubbed the Snapdragon 800), as well as 2GB of RAM.

Both the Kindle Fire HD 7-inch and 9-inch models contain a 1.5GHz with a dual-core processor. With the obvious increase in power and screen resolution, the HDX also boasts a slightly longer battery life, which is quite impressive.

Below is the basic exterior layout of your HDX Device:

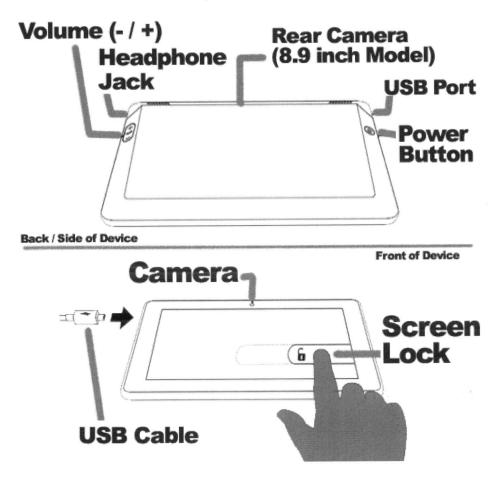

Back / Side of the HDX

Camera – The 8 Mega Pixel Rear Facing Camera is only available for the 8.9inch HDX model, capturing 1080p HD photos and videos.

Volume Buttons – There are two buttons on the back of your HDX to raise/lower the volume.

Headphone Input – You will find the input for your headphones next to the volume buttons.

Power Button – There is a power button on the back of your device, opposite the volume buttons.

USB Port – Next to the power button you will find the USB 2.0 Port.

Front Side of HDX

Camera – Both HDX models (7-inch and 8.9-inch have the 720 pixel HD front facing camera).

Lock Screen – When you press the power button, the lock screen display appears. Swipe the lock icon to the center of your screen to unlock the device, either powering it on or bringing it out of sleep mode. You may have to enter your lock screen password, if you've created one (see security settings).

Camera

The Kindle Fire HDX 8.9-inch is the first Kindle to have a rear-facing camera (the Kindle Fire HDX 7-inch and Kindle Fire HD 8.9 both have front-facing HD cameras, while the Kindle Fire HD 7-inch does not contain a camera).

Connectivity

Both HDX models offer 4G and dual-antenna Wi-Fi, whereas the Kindle Fire HD (7-inch) does not offer a 4G option, nor does it offer dual-antenna Wi-Fi. The Kindle Fire HD 8.9 offers 4G as an option.

Software

The Kindle Fire HDX (both models) and the Kindle Fire HD (7 inch) both come loaded with Kindle's new OS3 software. The Kindle Fire HD 8.9 does not have OS3 and Amazon has not announced if it will receive the update.

Weight

Obviously, weight is an important aspect for tablets since they are designed for mobile transport and use. The Kindle Fire HDX 7-inch with Wi-Fi Only weighs 303g. The Kindle Fire HDX 8.9-inch weighs 374g (which is 278g lighter than the iPad).

The Kindle Fire HD 8.9-inch weighs 567g, while the Kindle Fire HD 7-inch weighs 345g, so you can see how much lighter the newer models are. The HDX models allow for greater portability and ease of use.

Quick Start Guide

Turning on Your HDX for the First Time

The power button is located on the back of your device, at the bottom center. Hold down this button to turn on your device. The device boots up very quickly and will bring you to the lock screen. Swipe the lock icon from the side of the device to the center to unlock your screen.

First, you will be presented with a number of languages: select your desired language by tapping once on the screen. Then tap "Continue".

Next, you will then be asked to connect to a Wi-Fi network: select your local network by tapping once on the appropriate Wi-Fi connection. This will bring up the keyboard, prompting you to enter your password (if your network requires one). Type in your password and then press "Connect".

Next, the device will ask you to connect your social networks (Facebook and Twitter). You can choose to integrate these by tapping on "Connect Your Facebook Account" and/or "Connect Your Twitter Account". You will then be prompted to type in your username and password for the subsequent account. Connecting your profiles will allow for easy sharing of your content to these social networks.

If you do not wish to connect these, you can just tap "Next".

Finally, you will be taken to your main screen and be prompted with a "Get Started" option. Selecting this option guides you through the basic swipe gestures, including swiping left and right to view recently used apps, as well as swiping up to see your apps and content (this is called Grid View), and swiping back down to return to the main "Carousel".

Powering On/Off & Sleep Mode

To put your HDX into "Sleep" mode (which means it won't fully power down and can quickly be booted back up), simply tap the power button on the back of the device.

To power off the Kindle, hold the button down for a few seconds. A prompt will appear on your device's screen asking if you would like to turn off your device.

To power on your HDX, hold down the power button for a few seconds. A "Kindle Fire HDX" icon will appear when the device begins to power up. The boot-up time is less than 30 seconds for the HDX.

Registering Your Kindle Fire

Depending on who, how, or where your HDX was purchased, your device may already be linked to an Amazon account. This account is necessary for accessing your Amazon cloud, purchasing content directly on your device, and syncing all of your already owned content.

If your device is not yet registered you will need to link your Amazon account to your HDX.

First, make sure that you are connected to a wireless network. From your home screen swipe down to open the quick settings screen. Tap on the settings icon, and then tap on the My Account section from the settings screen. Now, just tap register.

You may already have an Amazon account if you purchased this device, or other items from Amazon. If you do have an account, enter your email address and password and then tap Register.

If you were gifted the device and do not have an Amazon account, tap Create Account and follow directions for setting up a new account on Amazon.

You have now connected your device to your Amazon account, which makes syncing your content extremely easy via your Amazon Cloud.

Deregister

You may wish to deregister your HDX if it is not registered to your account, or someone else is going to become owner of the device. Your device can only be registered to one account at a time, however you can have more than one device registered to your account. You can deregister your HDX from your computer or on the device itself.

If you are deregistering from your device, connect to a Wi-Fi network. From your Home screen swipe down from the top to open the Quick Settings screen. Tap on the Settings icon, and then tap on the My Account section from the settings screen. Now, just tap Deregister.

If you are deregistering from a computer, go to Amazon.com and log into your Amazon account. Navigate to your Manage Your Kindle page, found in the dropdown next to the search bar. From this page, click the Manage Your Devices tab (currently found in the left side navigation). From this page, find the HDX device you wish to deregister from your account. This means your device will be disconnected from your Amazon account and all of the content in your Amazon cloud will no longer be accessible on your HDX.

There will be a button/link that says deregister; click to deregister your HDX. You are now free to re-register your HDX to another Amazon account.

Navigating Your HDX

You will find navigating the HDX relatively easy and intuitive. The icons are bigger and easier to press than older models, and the main menu has been overhauled.

Rotating Your Screen

To change the display orientation, maneuver the device either so it's longer in height to view the screen in a portrait display or maneuver horizontally for landscape viewing of the screen.

In order for this to occur, the Auto-Rotate setting must be enabled via your Quick Settings screen. If the Auto-Rotate setting is disabled, the screen will lock to whichever orientation is currently showing (either landscape or portrait).

Navigating the Various Screens

Home Screen

After powering your device on or waking it from sleep mode, unlocking your device will take you to the Home Screen. The Home Screen, from top to bottom, consists of the Status Bar, Navigation Bar, Carousel, Home Screen Recommendations, and Grid View.

After unlocking your device (by swiping the lock button), you will arrive at the Main Navigation screen. Let's look at the various sections, starting from the top and working to the bottom of the device.

The top menu, or the Status Bar, is the first section appearing at the top of the screen. This thin black menu bar contains indicators including the name of the device, the time, Wi-Fi connection, and battery life. These indicators act as just a simple reference point for the current status of your device.

Here is the list of all possible indicators that can appear in your Status Bar:

Status Bar Indicators

Your Kindle Fire is fully charged.

Your Kindle Fire needs to be charged.

Your Kindle Fire is charging.

Bluetooth is on and paired with a compatible Bluetooth device.

Bluetooth is on, but not in range or paired with a compatible Bluetooth device.

A new notification has arrived.
The number of unread notifications will appear in the circle.

Quiet Time is on.

An app or a website is using Wi-Fi to estimate your device location

Parental controls are on.

Airplane Mode is on.

Your Kindle Fire is currently mirroring its screen.

Your Kindle Fire is connected to a Wi-Fi network (strong signal).

Your Kindle Fire is connected to a Wi-Fi network (weak signa).

Your Kindle Fire is connected to a Wi-Fi network,
but can't connect to the Internet.

Navigation Bar

Across the top of the screen is the main Navigation Bar. This has a number of options: Search, Shop, Games, Apps, Books, Music, Videos, Newsstand, Audiobooks, Web, Photos, Docs, and Offers. We'll look these various content libraries briefly here in the Quick Start Guide and go into greater detail about each one later on. Let's just quickly look at the Search function found by tapping on the magnifying glass icon positioned all the way on the left side of the navigation Bar.

Search

Clicking the Search Icon will bring up the Search Screen. The keyboard will appear and you can type in what you're searching for. Before tapping "Go" to initiate your start, you have the option of narrowing down where the search will take place. You can select from Libraries, Stores, and Web.

Selecting Libraries will initiate the search from within the content libraries of your device and other content as well, such as contacts. Selecting Stores will narrow your search query to just content found within the Amazon Marketplace. Selecting the web will open a search to the World Wide Web via a Google Browser.

Quick Tip: When you begin to type your query, your HDX will begin displaying smart search results based on what you are typing. There's a good chance that what your searching for, especially if within your libraries, will appear in these smart search results thus saving you time.

Carousel

The main Carousel is located in the middle (from left to right) – this lets you swipe through your recently used apps and items. This proves very convenient, making your Home Screen very helpful now that it stores your most recently used items.

Remove an item from Carousel – tap and hold the item in your carousel, and then select Remove From Carousel.

Home Screen Recommendations

Removing Recommendations

You may wish to remove individual recommendations from your Home Screen. To do so, just press and hold the recommendations you wish to remove and tap the Not Interested button. It will be removed and won't appear when scrolling through your carousel in the future.

You may wish to remove recommendations all together. To do so, swipe down from the top of the Home Screen. This will bring up your quick settings, and then you want to tap on the Settings icon. Find Applications and tap. Now, find the Home Screen option and tap on it. You can toggle the Show/Hide button to disable these recommendations from appearing.

Grid View

Below the Carousel and Home Screen recommendations (if enabled) appears your Home Screen Grid View. This contains items you wish to store for quick access from your Home Screen. By default, your HDX will place several apps and utilities in your Grid View.

To remove an item from Grid View, just press and hold the icon of the item. At the top of your screen, a Remove button appears. Tap to remove the item.

Throughout your content libraries you will come across items such as apps, games, documents, and utilities that you wish to appear in your Home Screen Grid View.

To add an item to Grid View, just press and hold the icon of the item. Three options will be appear and select the first option, "Add to Home".

Additional Screens

The quick settings screen is not displayed by default; you can access it by swiping down from the top of the screen.

You are now viewing the Quick Settings toolbar, which contains icons to just a few of the many settings found on your HDX (settings you will want to access more frequently).

When viewing the quick settings menu (see above), you will see these icons and be able to tap on each icon to adjust their settings.

The Settings icon all the way on the right will bring you to the main settings page where all of your settings can be accessed. We will look at all of those settings in greater detail in the next chapter.

For now, let's quickly look at what each of these quick settings controls and how you can best utilize the quick settings screen:

Auto-Rotate

This control allows you to lock your Kindle screen so that it does not switch from landscape to portrait view when you turn your device. Hold your device so the screen appears how you wish, and then simply tap the Auto-Rotate button to lock the screen. To enable auto-rotate again, just tap the button.

Brightness

This next control allows you to adjust the brightness of your device's screen. Depending on your viewing environment and which features you are using, this quick setting will be very handy and you can adjust the brightness by just sliding the circle tab left (to dim) and right (to brighten).

Additionally, you have the option of selecting Auto-Brightness. By turning this on, the device will adjust the brightness automatically depending on your environment. This feature will make it so even dark parts of an image become lighter so they aren't lost in bright light environments. This is a very helpful aspect of this feature, and should make auto-brightness the popular option for most people

Wireless

The next quick control is the Wireless settings. Within the Wireless setting, you can adjust airplane mode, select a Wi-Fi connection, enable Bluetooth, and adjust Location-Based Services.

Airplane Mode
You can toggle Airplane mode on/off. Disabling Airplane Mode will turn off your Wi-Fi connectivity. When you toggle Airplane Mode on, you will see a small airplane icon appear in the top menu next to your battery life indicator.

Wi-Fi
Tapping the Wi-Fi button will take you to the Wi-Fi settings page where you can turn Wi-Fi on/off. When turned on, you will see all the available Wi-Fi networks listed underneath where it says Wi-Fi networks. Select the network you wish to join, and enter the necessary password when prompted. It is highly suggested that you only connected to secure networks.

Bluetooth
Tapping the Bluetooth button will take you to the Bluetooth settings page where you can turn Bluetooth on/off. By turning

24

on Bluetooth, you can pair your Kindle HDX with another device. Once turned on, tap the Pair a Bluetooth Device button to bring up a list of available devices.

The Kindle HDX can pair up with a variety of devise such as keyboards, controllers, and A2DP compatible headsets, speakers, and headphones. The HDX does not offer NFC (near-field communications) Bluetooth connectivity. When you toggle Bluetooth on, you will see a small antenna like icon appear in the top menu next to your battery life indicator.

Location-Based Services
Toggling this setting on will prompt a pop up, "By enabling this feature, location data about your Kindle is sent to Amazon and third-party apps and websites..." in which by selecting "Continue" will turn on these services.

This simply allows third party integrations to use location data to better serve your search query needs and app usage. Tap this button again to turn off this setting.

Quiet Time

Tapping the Quiet Time button will enable "Quiet Time" which turns off all notifications. When quiet time is enabled, you will see a small icon of a circle with a minus sign in it appear in the Status Bar next to your device's name. Tap this button again to disable quiet time.

Mayday

Tapping the Mayday button from your Quick Settings screen will take you to the Amazon Assist main screen, containing the Mayday feature. Mayday is Amazon's new customer service feature that is available to help users navigate their device. Since Amazon's marketplace is highly integrated into the HDX, this feature is intended to help guide the user experience, assist in the buying experience, and act as an overall help center. We will explore this feature in greater detail later in this guide.

To enable Mayday, tap the yellow connect button and you will be connected to an Amazon customer service rep within 15 seconds (as noted by Amazon). This representative will be able to see what your screen is displaying, but will not see you nor your account information.

Settings

Tapping on last quick settings icon will take you to the main settings page, which is covered in great detail in the next chapter.

Notification Tray

While still looking at your Quick Settings screen, you can view your current list of notifications. You are able to modify and interact with these notifications directly from this screen.

Notifications are alerts that inform you of background tasks and activity occurring while you are currently using another app or viewing your media. For example, a new message in your Inbox could trigger a notification based on your settings.

For each notification, you can either tap on it to interact with it (e.g. view your email), or can swipe to dismiss the notification. You can dismiss all of your notifications by tapping Clear All.

*Turning on Quiet Time will mute sounds and hide notifications from appearing on your device. Just tap the Quiet Time icon from this same quick settings screen atop to turn on.

Options Bar

Every page, other the Home Screen, contains an Options Bar at the bottom of the screen:

Home Button (Bottom Left) – Takes you to the Home screen
Back Button (Bottom Middle) - Returns you to previous screen
Menu button (Bottom Middle) – Opens the current screen's menu for accessing additional settings
Search Button (Bottom Right) – Opens the search bar and the keyboard appears for executing your search.

*If you do not see an options bar, simply tap the middle of your device's screen.

Navigation Panel

When you are within one of your content libraries or some utilities such as the web browser, you can bring up an additional navigation panel with more options and quick links.

Simply swipe right from the left side of the screen to open the Navigation Panel, and swipe back left to hide it. Below is an example of the Navigation Panel found that appears when you are inside of the Amazon Store.

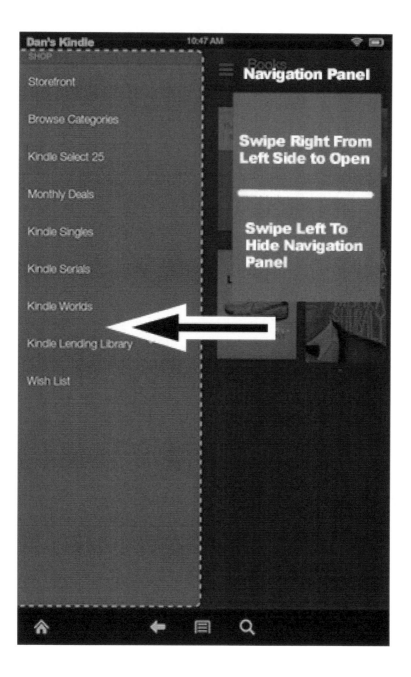

Unique Screens & Helpful Maneuvers

Within an Application

When you are inside of an application or have an eBook open, you can click in an empty space on the screen in order to bring up some additional options and your Options Bar. Depending on the app, you will get a toolbar across the top that gives you a number of options. For example, an open eBook will give you font options, bookmarks, etc.

Quick Switch

If you wish to open recent media you were using, it's best to make use of the Quick Switch bar. Simply swipe your finger upwards from the bottom Options Bar. A slider containing recently opened media appears and you can just tap on whichever app, book, or utility you wish to open.

For example, when reading a book, tap an empty space on the screen (as mentioned above), which will bring up the additional options and Options Bar. From here, swipe upwards and your recent applications will be revealed in a slider.

Swype to Type

When using your keyboard, you can use the integrated Swype feature to enter your text faster than ever. Just press down on the first letter of your word and then swipe to the next letter until you've completed spelling the word. Then release your finger and check to see if the word you've intended to type has appeared.

Swype will insert spaces as well, so just start swiping your next word and a space will be inserted.

Exploring the Amazon Store & Your Content Libraries

One of the cornerstones of the Kindle Fire HDX is its integration with the Amazon marketplace. You literally have millions of books, movies, TV shows, and physical products at your fingertips.

To bring up the Amazon Store, select "Shop" from the top-left side of the Navigation Bar on your Home Screen. You'll see a few options, including "Shop Amazon" for physical products, as well as "Books", "Videos", "Music", "Games", "Newsstand", "Apps", "Audiobooks", and "Amazon Prime" to shop various digital products. There will also be a carousel of suggested content and advertisements on the bottom of your screen, which you can scroll through by swiping to the left or right.

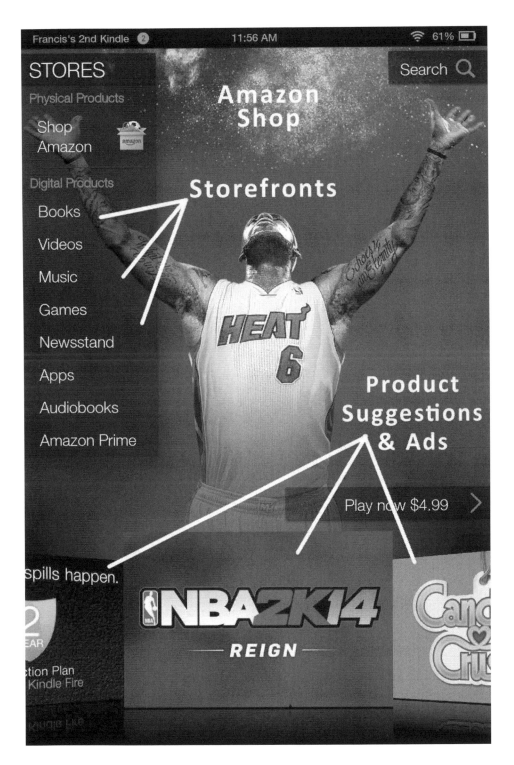

Once in the Amazon Store, select "Books" on the left hand side, to view the Book marketplace. If you have registered your device, it will already be synced with your Amazon account and will give you relevant suggestions. Here, you will see three rows of the suggestions. The top row is an alternating row of Best Sellers, Kindle Daily Deals, and other suggestions based on your browsing preferences and purchases.

The next is a row of "Recommended for You" books, which you can browse by swiping left or right. The bottom row is the "Kindle Select 25", which lists 25 exciting books for the week, curated by Amazon.

You can bring up more rows of suggestions by swiping up. Some of these categories include "Monthly Deals", "Best of the Year So Far", "Kindle Serials", and "New & Noteworthy". You can also search for books by tapping the magnifying glass icon in the upper right hand corner. This will bring up a search bar and the keyboard.

Once you select a book, it will bring you to the description page/listing page. This screen contains the details of the book, including a large cover image on the left, an option to purchase (the yellow bar), as well as a description of the book. If you scroll down, you will also see recommended books by customers who bought this book, as well as "Editorial Reviews" and "Customer Reviews". At the very bottom of the listing, you will see an "About the Author" page (if available) and "Product Details" including the page length, Publisher, and date released.

Purchasing Amazon Books

To purchase a book, select "Buy for (specified price)" from within the Book's description page/listing. Once your device is registered to your Amazon account, you won't need to fill in your payment account information, and the book will commence downloading (depending on your connection, this should only take a matter of seconds). You can then select "Read Now" to read it on the spot.

Adding Books to Your Wish List

On Amazon, you can build a "Wish List" to save books you are browsing that you may want to purchase in the future. To add a book to your wish list, first tap on the book listing on Amazon. Next, you will see a tab titled "More Options", directly beneath the yellow "Buy" tab. Tap "More Options", then tap "Add to Wish List" on the drop down menu. You will be asked if you would like to go to your Wish List. Select "View Wish List" to access your Wish List or select "Close" to continue browsing.

Navigating Your Content Libraries

The Kindle Fire HDX syncs seamlessly with your Amazon account. This means that all of the books, movies, and shows you have downloaded will be accessible on the device. You can also load items directly from you computer on to your HDX.

Book Library

To access your Book Library, select "Books" from the Navigation Bar at the top of your Home screen. You will see a grid of all the books that you have downloaded from Amazon. This is on your "Cloud", meaning you have at one time downloaded these books from Amazon, but they are not yet loaded on your device. Swipe up and down to scroll through your books.

Downloading Books from the Cloud

To download a book from your Cloud, first make sure you are in the "Cloud" tab, then, simply tap the desired book. This only takes a few short seconds; when the download is complete there will be a small check mark on the bottom right hand corner of the book. This book is now downloaded to your device and you can read it anywhere! Simply tap on the book and it will open instantly.

Browsing Books "On Your Device"

To browse only the titles that you have downloaded to your device, select "On Device" in the upper right hand corner, within your Book Library. This will show a grid of titles that are ready to read (most Kindle's come stocked with dictionaries for your desired language). To go back to all of your book purchases, select "Cloud" in the upper right hand corner.

Browsing the Books Library Menu

To bring up the Books Navigation Panel, from within the Books Library select the icon with the 3 parallel lines in the upper left hand corner of your device. This will bring up the Navigation Panel on the left side of your screen. Here, you can go to your Book Library, or go directly to the Amazon storefront, different sales categories, or your Wish List. You can also access your "Settings" menu from here. To access the Amazon store, select "Store" in the upper right hand corner of the screen.

TIP: Swipe from left to right from the far left side of the screen to quickly bring up the Books Library menu.

Music Library

To access the Music Library, select "Music" from the Navigation Bar at the top of the home screen. The first time you open the

Music Library, you will be presented with Amazon's "Terms of Use". Tap "Continue" to accept the terms of use, or tap the "Terms of Use" hyperlink within the text to view the terms of use.

Once on the device, you will be presented with two options: "Download from the Cloud" or "Transfer via USB". Select "Cloud" from the upper right hand corner to view music in your Amazon cloud. Select "On Device" in the upper right hand corner to view music that you have downloaded on to your device.

☰ Albums   Cloud   On Device   Store >

Cloud vs. Device

Shields
Grizzly Bear
10 songs

Tap for Album Details

Click for Navigation Panel

Albums Grid

When first using your device, you will not have any music downloaded on your device. Thus, the "On Device" section will read "No music on device". You may, however, have music on your Amazon cloud, which you can easily download onto your device. Tap "Cloud" from the upper right hand corner. You will see a grid with the Albums on your Cloud (if you previously stored music on your Amazon Cloud). To download, tap the desired album. This will bring you to the details screen for this album. If you are connected to Wi-Fi or 4G, you can play music directly from this page.

Playing Music

From within the Music Library, tap on an album. Now, select "Play All" at the bottom of the album cover to play the album in full. This will bring up another screen and will start playback on the album. You can control playback of your album. The bottom left hand side has 3 options: to go to the previous track, pause the track, or go to the next track.

The bottom right hand side has 3 more options from left to right: a repeat play option (to play the current track over again), a shuffle option (to randomly play tracks within this album after the current track), and a volume option (tap once to bring up the volume control). Then you can drag the dot up or down to adjust the volume. Select the arrow on the upper left hand corner of your screen to go back. This will bring you back to the higher-level view of your current album.

Download to Your Device

To download this album to your device, select "Download All" on the right hand side of the screen to download to your device. This will download this album to your device in the background. Once completed, you can access this album by selecting "On Device" in the upper right hand corner of your screen.

From the playback screen you can also select "Explore Artist" to access an Amazon page about the artist. This will give you some information about the artist, as well as similar artists and photos. Select the back button at the bottom of the screen to go back. Select the Home button at the bottom left hand corner to go back to the Home screen.

Video Library

To access your video library, select "Videos" from the top toolbar on the Home screen. This will bring you to a Videos page where you can purchase video content from Amazon (including TV shows and Movies). We will delve into purchasing videos later. To access your Library, select "Library" from the upper right hand corner of your screen.

This will bring you to a library very similar to the Books and Music Library. Upon first usage, you will likely have no videos on your device. You may have purchased videos on your Amazon account previously, which may be accessible by selecting "Cloud" in the upper right hand corner. From here, you can browse either "Movies" or "TV" by tapping one of these selections on the top center of the screen.

If you have movies or shows on your cloud, you will be presented with a grid-style view of your titles. Tap on a title to go to the listing page.

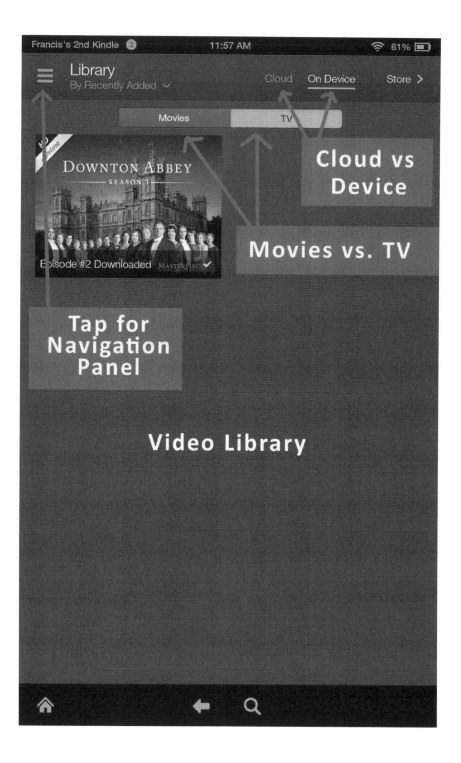

Francis's 2nd Kindle ② 11:57 AM 📶 61% 🔋

Library
By Recently Added ∨

Cloud   On Device   Store >

Movies   TV

DOWNTON ABBEY
SEASON 3

Episode #2 Downloaded MASTERPIECE ✓

Cloud vs Device

Movies vs. TV

Tap for Navigation Panel

Video Library

The listing page for TV shows will allow you to Play or Resume your latest episode (the green tab on the top), as well as add the show to your Wish List, or choose to purchase in HD or SD (standard definition). If you swipe up to scroll down, you can view the show's episodes by season and choose to download to your device or stream the episode. We'll talk more about purchasing video (including TV shows & Movies) later on.

Apps Library

The Amazon marketplace has thousands of Android applications that you can download to your device, all of them being tailored and optimized for the Kindle Fire HDX.

There are two ways to access your Apps Library. You can select "Apps" from the top toolbar or you can swipe up from the bottom of you Home screen to bring up the Grid View. For our purposes, select "Apps" from the top toolbar, as this will give us a more in-depth view.

You will be presented with a grid-style view of your downloaded apps, as well as those on your Cloud that you may have downloaded at one time on your Amazon account. The icons with the check mark in the lower right hand corner are the apps that are downloaded on your device and are ready for immediate use. Simply tap an app with a check mark to open the app instantly.

The stock apps included with the device are "Help", "Silk Browser", "Calendar", "Camera", "Settings", "Contacts", "Kindle FreeTime, and "Shop Amazon". You may have other apps listed, which are apps you previously downloaded via your Amazon account.

You can download these to your HDX by simply tapping on the desired app icon. This will download the app to your device normally within seconds (depending on the size of the app and the strength of your internet connection).

Select "On Device" located in the upper right hand corner to view the apps that you have physically downloaded to the device. These are apps you can use immediately. Select "Cloud" to view a grid of apps you have downloaded in the past.

Note: not all apps in the "Cloud" view are immediately accessible. You will have to download those without a check mark by simply tapping them once.

You can sort the App Content grid by recently used Apps or by alphabetical order. Tap "Apps" in the upper left hand corner. On the subsequent drop down menu, you can select either "By Recent" or "By Title". This will sort your apps accordingly.

Kindle Apps Store

If you select "Store" in the upper right hand corner, the HDX will bring you directly to the App store. Here, the device will present you with a number of "Featured Apps & Games", which is a list curated by Amazon, as well as "Recommended for You" Apps, based on your book interests and previous App purchases. We will go into more detail regarding the App store later on in the guide.

Battery

When you first open your HDX, the battery may not have a full charge. It is recommended that you fully charge the device before registering and setting it up. Use the USB cable / power adapter included with your device to charge your HDX; it takes 5 hours or less for your device to be fully charged.

*Using a different power adapter and cable may increase the length required to charge your device, so use the included power source accessories.

Plug in the USB end of the cable into the USB port found on the side of your HDX and connect the other end of your cable into the power adapter. Then just plug the adapter into a power outlet.

When charging, your HDX will display a lightening bolt icon in the status bar on the Home screen.

Battery Meter/Battery Life

The battery meter is located in the top right corner of the device (on the Status Bar). You should see a small battery shaped device with a solid block approximating the amount of battery power left. With the factory settings, the battery meter does not show an exact percentage in the status bar.

However, you can change this manually. Swipe down from the top of the device to bring up the Quick Settings menu. Tap "Settings", then tap Device. You should see an option to toggle "Show Battery Percentage in Status Bar". Tap the On/Off switch on the right to toggle this option. This can be helpful in letting you know *exactly* how much batter life is left.

Setting Up Wi-Fi

You likely already set-up your Wi-Fi connection when you booted up your device. However, if you have left your home and entered a new wireless network, the HDX will automatically pick-up new wireless networks.

To view a list of nearby networks, swipe down from the top of the screen to open the Quick Settings menu. From here, tap "Settings" in the upper right hand corner. Then, select "Wireless", then "Wi-Fi". You will see "Wi-Fi Networks" with a list of available networks. Select the network you would like to connect to.

The networks with a small lock on the lower right hand side are password protected and will require you to enter a password. Those without a lock are free to the public to join. If you select a free network the device will automatically connect. If you select a password-protected network, the device will prompt you to enter a password. The on-screen keyboard will automatically pop-up and allow you to enter a password. Select "Connect" when you are done to complete your connection to the network.

In the Wi-Fi settings menu, you can also choose to turn your Wi-Fi receiver on or off. Turning off Wi-Fi will help conserve battery, but you will not be able to download or purchase content, or browse the web.

How to Browse The Web

Silk is the Kindle Fire HDX's built-in browser, developed specifically for Kindle devices. Overall, this is a stable and well-integrated browser, and we recommend sticking with this and not using a 3rd party browser.

To open Silk, tap the "Silk Browser" icon directly from the Grid View at the bottom of the Home screen. The browser will open instantly with a new tab. As you can see, the browser lists your "Most Visited" sites. If you haven't visited any sites yet, it will list popular sites, such as Amazon, Facebook, Wikipedia, Bing, Yahoo, and YouTube. Simply tap a website once to visit it. To leave a website, select the "X" on the upper right hand side of the open tab (you will see one or more tabs across the top of the screen).

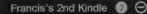
≡ New Tab **Tab** **New Tab** +

Enter search term or URL **Search Bar** 🔍

Most Visited

Amazon
Amazon.com: Amazon.com Gift Cards -...

Nytimes
The New York Times - Breaking News,...

Gutenberg.org
Pride and Prejudice by Jane Austen - Fr...

Bing
project gutenberg - Bing

Ebooks.nypl.org
The New York Public Library, eNYPL - L...

Nypl.org
eBooks, Digital Images & More | The Ne...

YouTube
Baby LED light suit halloween costume...

Secure42.libraryrese...
The New York Public Library, eNYPL - L...

Most Visited

Silk

To conduct a web search or enter a URL, tap the white search bar across the top of the screen (the bar reads "Enter search term or URL"). A keyboard will automatically pop-up at the bottom of the screen, as well as a list of your most recently visited sites. Type in your desired URL if you want to go to a specific website. To conduct a web search, simply type in a search term, such as "Kindle Fire HDX", then tap "Go" in the bottom right corner to complete the search.

Note: Silk will automatically conduct a search using Bing.com. We will show you how to change this in the "Browsing the Internet" section of the guide.

To leave the browser, select "Home" in the bottom right hand corner.

Advanced Settings

Settings Screen

The main settings screen contains access and information to every setting on your device. Tap the Settings icon from the quick settings screen to view all settings:

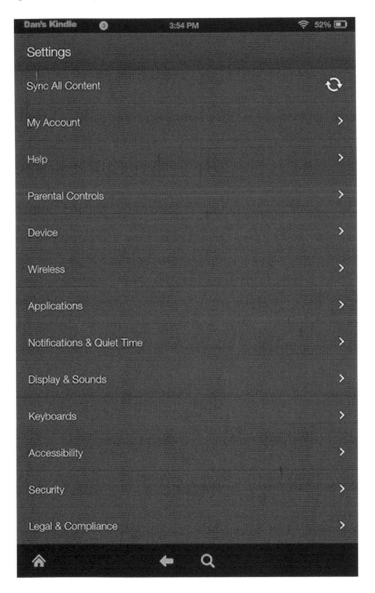

Sync All Content

This first setting provides you a quick option for syncing your HDX device to receive all of the content from your Amazon Cloud. Tap this button to sync all of your media including your books, games, audiobooks, and videos from your cloud to your HDX. This will even sync videos from where you've left off watching so you can continue watching from where you left off, right on your HDX.

My Account

The next setting listed is My Account, which contains all of your account information. In the quick start guide, we went through the required steps for connecting your Kindle Device to your Amazon Account.

Listed on this page is your device's registration information including the name you've given your device, your name, and your Kindle Email address.

Your Kindle Email address is a unique email given to your device once registered. This email is useful because it allows you and authorized users to send documents directly to your Kindle cloud account. Your kindle email address should look something similar to this: name@kindle.com or contact_4855@kindle.com.

Deregister Your Device

Tap the Deregister button to prompt a popup second screen. It will ask you if you wish to deregister your Kindle. By doing so, it will be no longer associated with your Amazon account, removing content from your device.

Your purchases from the Amazon Store will still remain available and for use or re-download in the Amazon Cloud. Only after confirming deregistration of the device can you can re-register your HDX to another Amazon account.

Your Account Settings

For the settings listed below the Deregister button, you will be prompted to enter in your Amazon account login information. This prompt will occur if you click on one of these five settings listed below. You should not have to re-enter your account information when looking at each setting, just enter once to can adjust all settings.

Account Settings
This option allows you to change the name, email, and password associated with the account.

Current country
You can change the country associated with your Kindle account here. If you are moving out of the country, this is where you can change your setting so your account is synced with the proper Amazon marketplace and web properties. It takes up to 30 minutes for a country change to take place.

Payment Options
There are two payment options that you can adjust. The first option, 1-Click Payment, allows you to select your payment method for your default 1-click purchases. All Kindle transactions utilize the 1-click checkout, so you must have an active credit or debit card on file. You can change your payment method at any time, but any ongoing subscriptions via the Kindle store will continue to charge the original credit card. Therefore, you will want to make the proper adjustments to your ongoing subscriptions before switching payment methods. This leads us to the next account setting, subscriptions.

Subscriptions

The subscriptions settings page allows you to view and manage your active subscriptions. These are paid subscriptions currently available on your account and include Magazine and Blog subscriptions.

Social Network Accounts
You can connect your Facebook and Twitter accounts to your HDX. Tap either to bring up a screen where you can enter in your account and password information. Once connected with your device, you will be able to easily share photos, content, passages from books, and more with your friends/family/followers.

Help (Amazon Assist)

Tapping the help setting brings you to your HDX's help center, also known as Amazon Assist; contains the new Mayday feature, as well as quick access to several helpful sections.

Using Mayday

Mayday is Amazon's new customer service feature that is available to help users navigate their device. Since Amazon's marketplace is highly integrated into it's tablet devices, this feature is intended to help guide the user experience, assist in the buying experience, and act as an overall help center.

To enable Mayday, tap the yellow connect button and you will be connected to an Amazon tech advisor. You will be connected within 15 seconds (as noted by Amazon). This advisor will be able to see what your screen is displaying, but will not see you nor your account information. You will be able to see advisor live on your HDX screen.

This advisor will guide you through any feature on your HDX and can even draw on the screen. They will walk you through step-by-step on how to do something or even do it for you.

Mayday assistance is available at all times, 24/7/365, and is absolutely free for U.S. customers. Currently, there are only English speaking agents on call. Mayday works best when you have a strong Wi-Fi connection.

Other Amazon Assist Features

Below the Mayday feature, you will find three icons: wireless, user guide, and contact us.

Tapping the wireless icon will bring up instructions for helping you setup wireless and/or Bluetooth connections. Included in this section are a few troubleshooting walkthroughs to help if you can't connect your device to a Wi-Fi or Bluetooth network.

Tapping the User Guide icon will bring up the default user guide that comes with every HDX. There is helpful information covering basic navigation and use of the features and is a great reference when you need to quickly recall what a certain feature is and how to access it.

A navigation panel is also accessible from the Amazon Assist home screen. Swipe the screen right or tap the top left icon next to Amazon Assist to pull this panel into view. This sidebar contains tabs for three icons just mentioned, as well as a few generic contact links.

Parental Controls

Within parental controls you will find it broken into two sections: 8 and under, and 9 and up. The first section in parental controls is simply a shortcut icon to access Kindle Free Time, the newly featured application offered by Amazon. This app allows creation of user profiles for children with suggested ages from 3 to 8 years old.

This feature was created to give device owners a way of controlling viewing permissions of content found on the device. When activated, this app provides a unique operating environment where users can only access media and content as defined by the owner of device.

Looking below the Kindle FreeTime app, you will find the parental controls for those 9 and up. Ultimately, these settings control the entire operating environment for HDX device. Amazon just titled the section "9 and up" to distinguish these controls from the Kindle FreeTime app. As owner of the device, you control the entire user experience in terms of purchasing control, blocking content types, e-mail, web browsing, and more.

Kindle FreeTime

Let's first look at Kindle Free Time, where profiles can be created for children using the device.

Amazon recommends creating profiles for children ages 3 to 8 years of age because they offer a premium subscription service, FreeTime Unlimited, which contains preloaded media, games, and books for children this age.

* FreeTime Unlimited is not required as you can still segment all of your purchased content for various users.

To get started, tap the icon and you will arrive in the Kindle FreeTime app where you can register a user account, which is completely free to do.

You can subscribe each profile for Kindle FreeTime Unlimited, which provides unlimited access to thousands of popular games, books, apps, and shows specifically for children. For now, let's just look at the registration process for setting up your basic profiles within the app.

Tap the Get Started button from the bottom of the Kindle Free Time app home screen. You will be prompted to enter your Parental Controls Password. If you have yet to create one (covered in the next part), you can create one at this point. Once you've entered/created your password, the Add Child Profile page will appear.

Here, you can enter in the name of the child, birthdate, gender, and even add a cute dinosaur, cat, or other picture to be associated with the account. Once filled out, tap Next. You will then arrive at the Manage Content & Subscription page where you will find your newly created user profile.

Tap the user profile to access the media for which this user can view. There will be a dropdown menu containing all of the various types of media, including one tab title "All". Tapping "All" will bring up all of the content downloaded on your Kindle Device.

Next to each book, movie, or app, you can tap on the checkbox to approve that content to be share with this user. Once you are done designating which content can be shared, tap the "Done" button at the top right of the screen. You will be taken back to the Manage Content & Subscription page where you will now see a quick count next to the user's name of how many books, videos, apps, etc. that they have access to.

Tap the back button to revisit the Add Child Profile page where you can add another user, or hit the home button if you're done creating profiles.

When you wish to pass your HDX off to a child user, simply open the user profile you've made for them from within the Kindle Free Time app. Open the Kindle FreeTime App and tap on the profile you wish to activate. Once opened, the app cannot be exited without entering in the parental controls password.

Several additional settings listed underneath the profiles for which you can adjust:

Manage Child Profiles – This tab takes you to settings page where you can register another child profile. You can edit details of current profiles, delete profiles, and adjust the daily time limits for that user.

Manage Content & Subscriptions – This tab will bring up a screen giving you the options to select a current profile to adjust media access, and also a shortcut to the FreeTime Unlimited service where you can subscribe/edit your settings.

Daily Time Limits – This tab allows you to set time limits for each user; you can control how much time they can spend on the device and in what fashion they spend their time.

First, you can toggle Time Limits On/Off. If toggled on, you have two options for setting time limits. You can limit the total screen time anywhere from 15 minutes to 6 hours.

Second, you can limit time by activity, where you can designate certain time amounts for certain activities including reading, watching videos, and using apps. Adjustments range from completely blocking certain activities to approving unlimited use of such activity.

More - This tab contains the three settings just mentioned above as well as a few other shortcuts, relevant for this app. You will find a tab that will take you to the Wireless & Networks settings as you may be strapping your children into their seats for a road trip and needing to quickly activate Bluetooth or 4G reception.

Parental Controls is also listed as this allows you to quickly change your parental controls password. Also included is a Help tab, which takes you to an informational page about Kindle Free Time. In addition, there's a feedback tab where you can leave feedback about FreeTime.

Exit - Lastly, there's an exit tab to tap for when you wish to leave the Kindle FreeTime app.

Parental Controls

With younger users profiles established within the Kindle Free Time app environment, it's now time to establish the controls for users utilizing all of the HDX's features such as purchasing and web browsing.

First, below Kindle FreeTime, you will see the toggle On/Off toggle for Parental Controls. Toggle this button on and you will be asked to setup and confirm a password. Enter in the password you desire twice and tap Submit.

*Note - Turning on Parental Controls will trigger a lock icon to appear in your Status Bar.

Once turned on, you can toggle the blocked/unblocked button to restrict use of the following activities:

Web Browsing – Blocks use of the web.
Email, Contacts, Calendars – Blocks use of these utilities.
Social Sharing – Blocks use of sharing via your Facebook/Twitter accounts synced to your device.
Camera – Blocks use of the camera.

*Note: Activity will be restricted when the button is yellow and reads "Blocked".

Below these 4 settings, you will find settings for:

Password Protecting Purchases – Toggle On/Off to require the parental control password to be entered when purchasing content from the Amazon Store or Amazon Shop app.

Password Protecting Video Playback – Require the parental control password to be entered before viewing of a video.

Block and Unblock Content Types – Tap this button to bring up a screen of all content types in which you can block each type. These content types include Newsstand, Books & Audiobooks, Music, Video, Docs, Apps & Games, and Photos. Toggle the block/unblocked button to restrict these content types. Tap the back button to return to the Parental Controls setting page.

Change Password – Tap this if you wish to change the Parental Controls password. This requires knowledge of the current password in order for a new password to be accepted.

Password Protect Wi-Fi – This requires entering of the password before turning on Wi-Fi.

Password Protect LBS – This requires entering of the password when turning on Location-Based Services.

Device

This next setting page contains all of your device specific information and hardware data.

Battery Meter – See the % of battery life remaining on your device.

Show Battery Percentage in Status Bar – Toggle this setting on/off to display the battery indicator in your status bar.

System Updates – Tapping this will bring you to an updates page where you can check to see if there are any system updates available. Tap the check now button to find out. Either new updates will be available and can be activated (check) or no updates will be found. It's important to visit this setting every now and then for new updates.

Language – Tapping this will bring you to a list of languages for which you can select from as to dictate the language your HDX will operate in.

Text-to-Speech – You can set the language and voice of your device's Text-to-Speech default reader, which will be put to use when using any application with this feature.

Date & Time – Tapping this will bring you to a settings page for your device's date and time settings. All you have to do is select your time zone from the list of options and that will dictate the time and date listed. The only other option you have on this page is to toggle on/off the 24-hour format for displaying time.

Storage – This page displays how much memory your device is utilizing to store your media. It is sub-categorized into 12 types of data storage, e.g. Photos or Books. Tapping into any of these sub categories will show you a complete list of your content with the amount of memory required to store each file. You can delete files from your HDX directly from this screen by tapping the checkbox next to the desired file and then tapping delete at the bottom of the screen.

Enable ADB – By default, this setting is turned off as it not safe to have it enabled; your Kindle and personal data will be unsecure. Leave this off unless you are a developer looking to test an app on your device.

Serial Number – A quick reference point to access your device's serial number if needed for purchase and warranty details.

Reset to Factory Defaults – This button allows you restore your HDX to its original default settings. Doing so removes your personal information and content downloaded to the device.

The Wireless setting, you can adjust airplane mode, select to a Wi-Fi connection, enable Bluetooth, and adjust Location-Based Services.

Airplane Mode

You can toggle Airplane mode on/off. Disabling Airplane Mode will turn off your Wi-Fi connectivity. When you toggle Airplane Mode on, you will see a small airplane icon appear in the top menu next to your battery life indicator.

Wi-Fi

Tapping the Wi-Fi button will take you to the Wi-Fi settings page where you can turn Wi-Fi On/Off. When turned on, you will see all the available Wi-Fi networks listed underneath where it says Wi-Fi networks. Select the network you wish to join, and enter the necessary password when prompted. It is highly suggested that you only connected to secure networks.

Bluetooth

Tapping the Bluetooth button will take you to the Bluetooth settings page where you can turn Bluetooth On/Off. By turning on Bluetooth, you can pair your Kindle HDX with another device. Once turned on, tap the Pair a Bluetooth Device button to bring up a list of available devices.

The Kindle HDX can pair up with a variety of devise such as keyboards, controllers, and A2DP compatible headsets, speakers, and headphones. The HDX does not offer NFC (near-field communications) Bluetooth connectivity. When you toggle Bluetooth on, you will see a small antenna like icon appear at the top of the screen (in the Status Bar) next to your battery life indicator.

Location-Based Services

Toggling this setting on will prompt a pop up, "By enabling this feature, location data about your Kindle is sent to Amazon and third-party apps and websites…" in which by selecting "Continue" will turn on these services.

This simply allows third party integrations to use location data to better serve your search query needs and app usage. Tap this button again to turn off this setting.

Applications

This is the settings page that contains all of your currently installed applications.

Apps from Unknown Sources

Toggle this On/Off to allow applications not from the Amazon Appstore to be installed. Toggling this "On" is not recommended as your Kindle and personal data becomes less secure. Use with caution.

Collect App Usage Data

This toggles On/Off Amazon's ability to collect data on your app experience, such as the frequency and duration of use of various downloaded apps from the Amazon App Store. Disallowing Amazon to collect this data will not affect your device or usage, it simply blocks Amazon from collecting data that may better prompt them to suggest content you may be interested.

Manage All Applications

Tapping this button will bring you to a page that houses all of your currently installed applications; not just apps, but every application used for allowing your HDX to run smoothly.

Tapping into any of these applications will bring up an informational screen for that application. You will be able to see the App name, storage/memory required for that application, cache captured, and permissions given to the app.

You have the ability to "Force stop" the app as well. This would prove useful if your device is experiencing problems due to a certain application that is running. It is recommended that you use the Mayday feature to contact an Amazon customer service representative before making adjustments on your own.

Amazon Applications

This last area contains Amazon applications running on your HDX that have more granular setting controls. There are 11 applications listed; tap on any of the listed apps to take you to its unique settings screen. Most of these settings screens can be accessed from the navigation panel when using the app, rather than navigating through these various settings screens to find the app you are looking for.

Notifications & Quiet Time

Quiet Time

This setting combines both your notification settings and the settings for the new Quiet Time feature. Tap the Quiet Time button to access the settings.

Temporary Quiet Time
You can toggle the Temporary Quiet Time On/Off, which is the same setting you can access from the Quick Settings menu.

Scheduled Quiet Time
Turn on Quiet time whenever you are involved in an activity:

This allows you to set Quiet Time to activate during certain activities. By tapping the checkboxes listed next to the various activities, you can enable/disable Quiet Time to occur during each activity. You can enable/disable Quiet Time for when you are engaging in the following activities: watching movies or TV, reading books, magazines, or newspapers, listening to audiobooks or MP3s, or Browsing in Silk.

Turn on Quiet Time on a schedule each day:
This allows you to schedule a time during everyday where your device will be in Quiet Time mode.

Notifications

Below Quiet Time, you will find the complete list of your Applications. You can tap on each application to bring up its notification settings. Depending on the application, there will be various notification settings you can control. Each application will offer just two notification settings to control.

First, you can control whether the applications notifications will show in your notification tray. These notifications are found below the Quick Setting bar on the Quick Settings screen.

Second, you can control if the notification will play a sound. These sounds of course will only play if your volume is on.

*Both can be toggled On/Off, but if you turn off the first notification setting which controls if they appear in the notification trey, sounds will also be turned off.

Display & Sounds

Volume
This slider bar allows you to adjust the volume of all media on your device. *Note – you can alternatively use the volume controls on the back of the device to adjust volume.

Notification Sound
Tap on this setting to find a selection of various sounds you can sample and choose from to be your default sound. Tap the sound you wish to set as your default sound.

Auto Brightness
Also found in the quick settings menu, you can control the auto brightness setting by toggling On/Off.

Display Brightness
If ignoring the auto brightness, use this slider to adjust the brightness of your screen.

Display Mirroring

This setting allows you to wirelessly duplicate your HDX screen and audio onto another screen, such as a compatible HD TV or other media-streaming device. Your HD TV or streaming device must be Miracast-compatible, which you can find out by reading through your device's user guide.

If not compatible, you can use an HDMI adapter to connect your HDX with your HD TV. The HDX does not have an HDMI port so you will need an adapter, such as the NETGEAR Push2TV Wireless Display HDMI Adapter – Miracast and WiDi (PTV3000) http://www.amazon.com/gp/product/B00904JILO/.

This will connect to your TV and then you will be able to wirelessly connect to this adapter and stream your HDX media.

Enable Mirroring

First, you have to ensure that your device is "discoverable" in order for the HDX to recognize your streaming device wirelessly. Enabling your device so that it is discoverable varies across each device so check with your device's user guide for steps on how to do so.

Next, head to your settings page via the Quick Settings screen by swiping down from the top of your screen. Here, you will find the Display & Sounds menu, tap to open and then tap Display Mirroring. Your HDX will look for "discoverable" devices and list them accordingly. Find your device, and tap Connect.

This process can take up to 20 seconds to complete. Successful mirroring will result in your display and audio being outputted on the other device. Additionally, under your device's name you will see "mirroring". Just tap Stop Mirroring to end the connection.

Display Sleep

Tapping this setting brings you to a settings page where you can choose the duration before your HDX screen goes to sleep. Selecting a shorter duration length will extend your battery life, and visa versa.

Keyboards

These settings are made available to you for adjusting your on-screen keyboard that appears when prompted to type.

Languages

Tapping this allows you to set the default language for your keyboard. By default, your device comes preloaded with various languages. You can see the list of active keyboard languages on this screen. Tap on Default Language and then set whichever language you'd like to be your default keyboard language.

You can download more languages by tapping on the Download Languages button. You will be given a huge list to choose from.

Select your desired language, accept the terms of service, and the language will be installed to your device. From there, you can set it to be your Default Language.

Keyboard Settings

Sound on keypress – Toggle On/Off for sounds to occur when typing on keyboard.

Auto-correction – Toggle On/Off for automatically correcting typos.

Auto-capitalization – Toggle On/Off for assisted capitalization to occur.

Next word prediction – Toggle On/Off for words to be predicted based on previous text.

Check Spelling – Toggle On/Off for spelling errors to be marked.

Personal Dictionary - Words added to your personal dictionary will appear on this screen. These are suggested words that have appeared atop your keyboard when typing and that you have clicked on. You can delete these words individually or by selecting all and then tapping "Delete".

Bluetooth Keyboard

If you've paired a Bluetooth keyboard to your HDX these are the keyboard settings that apply.

Language – Set your default language by tapping the language you desire.
Bluetooth Keyboard Shortcuts – With your Bluetooth keyboard connected, you will be given a list of keyboard shortcuts you can use to help you type more efficiently.

Accessibility

Accessibility features allow you to navigate your device utilizing certain gestures and also hear audible feedback on items you've touched/opened. These features are intended for only a small portion of users and requires extensive documentation, of which is provided by Amazon's tutorial within the HDX.

Here is the link to Amazon's documentation on their website: http://amzn.to/1aJRh8R

Security

Lock Screen – You can toggle On/Off to set a mandatory password for accessing your device. Tap this button to turn this security feature on; you will then be prompted to enter a numeric PIN as your password. It must be four characters long and entered twice for confirmation. Tap finish when done.

Once a lock screen password is entered, you can change the password in the setting below. Tap the button to prompt a screen for entering a new password. You will have to enter this new password in twice and also enter in the old password.

Require Lock Screen – Again, with a lock screen password enabled, you can tap on this setting to control when the lock screen appears after your device goes to sleep. By default, your screen will lock every time your device goes to sleep, however you can change this setting so that your device will remain unlocked for up to 30 minutes after being set to sleep before requiring the password to be entered again.

Credential Storage & Device Administrators

*These two settings are not intended for consumers, but for enterprise applications.

You can view four legal and compliance standards pertinent to
your HDX Device:
Legal Notices, Terms of Use, Safety and Compliance, Privacy.

Tap on any of these 4 options to be taken to the appropriate legal
document. You may have to select the country for which you live
in to view the proper documentation. This section acts simply as
a quick reference point for Amazon to list and link to it's various
legal documents.

Downloading, Syncing, and Sending

Amazon's Cloud Services & Your HDX

Accessing your Amazon Cloud is discussed throughout this guide as it plays a major role in the syncing of your media, content, apps, and subscriptions.

Amazon's Cloud services refers to the wide variety of cloud storage services they provide. New services are constantly being introduced, while older services are expanding. Don't be overwhelmed by the terminology and variations of the word "cloud". Ultimately, these cloud services provide a safe and easy to access storage point for all of your content, regardless of if the content is a movie purchased on Amazon or a personal document you produced in Microsoft Word.

With purchase of your Kindle Fire HDX, you receive free and unlimited storage for all of your Amazon Purchased content and 5GB of free storage for personal documents, videos, music, photos. Additional storage can be purchased if needed.

With unlimited storage for Amazon content and tons of storage for personal documents, the cloud is where you will store much of your content. You can elect to sync your cloud with your HDX so that both contain the same content, but since your HDX has limited room you may wish to select only the content and media you want to have access to from your device.

Where's Your Cloud Content

From within any of your HDX's content libraries, you will find an On Device tab & Cloud tab at the top of your screen. Tap on the Cloud to view all of your content.

Syncing Content Between Cloud and Your HDX

Once you connect to a wireless network, you can sync your HDX so that it receives your content from the Cloud. Not only will your content become available on your HDX, but your progress within books, videos, and app updates will also synchronize.

Syncing Everything

The easiest way is to visit your settings screen, which can be accessed from the Quick Settings menu by swiping down from the top of your Home screen. From the Settings screen, tap the Sync All Content button for your content to sync from your Cloud to your HDX.

Note: This will merely sync your Cloud content on your HDX with the content on your Amazon Cloud. It will *not* download all of your Amazon Cloud content to your device.

Downloading Individual Content From Your Cloud

You may wish to download certain media and content from your Cloud to your HDX. To actually place your newly purchased content or files on your device, you must first connect to a wireless network. On the Home screen, select whichever Kindle content library contains your purchase. (e.g. Visit your Book Library if you've just purchased a Kindle book).

Once you've found the recently purchased item, simply tap to download. Already downloaded items will show a checkmark in the bottom right side of the image and items without a checkmark are only stored in the cloud.

Transfer via USB

You can easily transfer content from your computer to your Kindle Fire HDX. First, use the micro-USB cable that came with the device to hook-up your HDX to your computer.

Mac users will need to download an "Android File Transfer" application on their computer. Go to

Kindle.com/support/downloads to follow the directions and download this. Once you download and install this, you are ready to transfer files.

Windows XP users will need to install the latest version of Windows Media Player in order to transfer files.

If you are using a PC, your USB storage will be mounted as a drive in the Computer or My Computer section. You can drag files from your PC into this drive, just as you would any other drive. Once you are finished, eject the device from your Windows file browser before unplugging.

If you are using a Mac, open your "Android File Transfer" program on your computer. Here, you will see a series of folders. These are folders within your Kindle Fire HDX.

Locate the files on your computer that you would like to transfer. Now drag these files or folders into the relevant folder within the Kindle's USB drive. For example, if you are transferring music, drag the files into the "Music" folder. Depending on the file sizes, they may take anywhere from a few seconds to nearly an hour (if you are uploading say some movies or an entire music collection).

To disconnect your Kindle, open the file manager and select "Eject Android File Transfer". You are now free to disconnect the device from your computer.

Quick Tip: Video content (including Movies & TV Shows) that you transfer from your computer to your Kindle may be listed within your "Photos" content library.

Quick Tip: You can easily send content from your Kindle to your computer. When logged into your account on Amazon.com, locate "Manage Your Kindle", which is under the "Your Account" menu on the upper right hand side. To the right of each piece of content, you will see "Actions". Hover over this and choose

"Download & Transfer via USB". You can then choose your device and click "Download" to save content to your computer.

Below are file types that are compatible with your Kindle Fire HDX:

Audiobooks: AAX, AA
Books: MOBI, AZW (.azw3), KF8
Documents: TXT, PDF, PRC, DOCX, DOC
Music: E-AC-3 (Dolby Digital Plus), AC-3 (Dolby Digital), MP3, AAC (.m4a), OGG, MIDI, MP4, WAV, AAC LC/LTP, HE-AACv2, HE-AACv1, AMR-WB, AMR, NB
Pictures: JPEG, GIF, PNG, BMP
Movies: MP4, 3GP, VP8 (with video playback at 720p)

Removing Content

Removing Content From HDX

With limited storage space on your device, you may wish to remove content from your HDX. Within your settings screen tap on Device and then tap on Storage. Here you will find the various types of content stored on your device – tap on any category to view the files and the corresponding memory needed. Just tap on the file's checkbox and then tap remove from HDX.

Removing Content From Cloud (Permanent)

You can also remove content from the Cloud. When you do this, it will be permanently deleted (unlike deleting from your HDX). You can easily do this by pressing and holding on an item within one of your Content Libraries. (Make sure you are in the "Cloud" tab). You will see "Delete from Cloud". Tap this to delete the item permanently.

Your Kindle HDX will be assigned a "Send-to-Kindle" email address. This email address allows for documents to be sent from approved email accounts. Once sent, these documents will be added to your Kindle HDX and Cloud. Every Kindle device and free Kindle reading apps is assigned their own Send-to-Kindle email address for this purpose.

You can retrieve your Send-to-Kindle email from the Manage Your Devices page within your Amazon account. It will look something similar to: contact_4855@kindle.com.

Sending Documents

To find your Send-to-Kindle e-mail address, first go to Amazon.com. Find the Manage your Devices page within Manage Your Kindle (this will be to the right of the search bar). Next, find and click the Personal Document Settings page found in the left side navigation of your Manage your Devices page.

This page allows you to add new approved email addresses by clicking the button on the bottom of the page. All approved email addresses will now be able to send documents by simply emailing your Send-to-Kindle email address and attaching approved file types to the email.

Quick Tip: No subject line is required, however, adding "convert" as your subject line will trigger Amazon to convert any PDF file into an Amazon file (.azw). This allows you to take advantage of advanced features when you view your files such as altering font size, adding annotations, and Whispersync.

Received documents will also be added to your Cloud account, with Amazon providing free memory of up to 5GB. You can disable this setting from your Personal Document Settings page so files will not store on your Cloud.

*Note – Service fees are assessed when using this feature and NOT using Wi-Fi.

Additional Information:

Amazon is always adjusting this feature in regards to files types, file sizes, and additional service fee structures. It is best that you view the most updated information on this feature if you intent on using it. You can view more information here - http://amzn.to/1csW43W

Send-To-Kindle Application

Additionally, you can download and install the Send-To-Kindle application.

http://www.amazon.com/gp/sendtokindle

This app will allow you to quickly send your personal documents to your Kindle HDX. It currently is available for desktops (either Mac or PC), Android devices, and for web browsers in the form of an extension (Google and Firefox).

The Sent-to-Kindle's one-click feature makes it extremely easy to send articles from your computer to your devices and cloud. These articles are automatically Kindle-formatted and ready to read when sent.

Amazon Prime

What is Amazon Prime?

Amazon Prime is a membership program offered by Amazon that gives you free two-day shipping on most products, access to instant streaming of over 41,000 moves and television episodes, as well as the ability to borrow eBooks free of charge from a selection of more than 350,000. There is also no minimum order size needed to redeem your free two-day shipping. You will receive one free borrow each month, which you can use for books within the Kindle Owners' Lending Library.

Normally, Amazon Prime is $79 per year. However, with your Kindle Fire HDX purchase, you will receive a free month of Amazon Prime. This free month will start once you activate your Kindle; you will immediately be able to access Amazon Prime content.

The beauty of the Kindle Fire HDX is that it integrates seamlessly with your Amazon Prime account. You can now download Prime Instant Video shows and movies for free, which you can then watch on-the-go, without needing an internet connection. You can also stream Amazon Prime moves and TV shows with an Internet connection, without needing to download them to your device. All Prime Instant Video content is free of commercials.

Borrowing Books for Free From the Kindle Owners' Lending Library

For an avid reader, Amazon Prime is an asset, as it allows you to borrow one free book per month from the Kindle Owners' Lending Library. According to Amazon, there are over 350,000 books available for free borrow, including all-time best sellers such as the Harry Potter series, Hunger Games, and a number of Kurt Vonnegut novels (among many others).

However, we must note that it is unlikely the majority of your favorite books and authors will be available for free borrowing. While 350,000 books is more books than anyone can read, it is a drop in the ocean of books available on Amazon. If you opt-into Amazon Prime expecting to download a new book from your favorite author - say Stephen King – every month, you may be disappointed.

However, you can browse the Kindle Owners' Lending Library for many interesting best-selling titles, as well as countless self-published titles. (Amazon encourages self-published authors to opt their books into the Kindle Owners' Lending Library).

Browsing the Kindle Owners' Lending Library

To access the Kindle Owners' Lending Library as an Amazon Prime member, select "Shop" from the Home screen. Then select "Books" from the side menu. Now, tap the icon with 3 parallel lines in the upper left hand corner (the Navigation Panel will slide out from the side). Tap "Kindle Lending Library".

Now you're in the Kindle Lending Library. All of these books are available for FREE via borrowing. But choose wisely, as you will only have 1 borrow per month!

To borrow a book, tap on the book listing within the store. Now, tap "Borrow for Free", which is located under the yellow "Buy" tab. The book will download and you will now be able to read the book, free of charge!

Prime Instant Video

According to Amazon, there are over 41,000 movies and TV shows available for free as a member of Amazon Prime. For example, some popular TV shows include Duck Dynasty,

Downton Abbey, Parks and Recreation, SpongeBob SquarePants, and Arrested Development, among many others.

There are also thousands of well-known movies available to stream for free via Amazon Prime, including Marvel's Avengers, The Italian Job, Thor, Hook, and many others (including hundreds of HD movies). You can easily stream or download any of these movies to your device for free.

Browsing Prime Instant Video

To access Amazon Prime eligible movies and shows, tap "Shop" on the upper left hand side of Home screen, then tap "Videos" under the "Digital Products" category. Here, you may see a "Recently Added to Prime" category, which you can browse by swiping left or right. All of these are available to stream or download for free.

To get access ALL of the Prime Movies & Shows, tap the 3 parallel line icon in the upper left hand side of your screen. Here, you will see "Prime Instant Videos", with 3 options underneath it: "Prime TV Shows", "Prime Movies", and "For the Kids". These all contain solely Prime content that you can stream and download for free.

To take a look, select "Prime TV Shows". Now you can swipe up and down to browse Prime eligible TV-shows. Select a show of your choice to enter the show's main listing. If you scroll down, you will see a horizontal list of all available seasons, with subsequent episodes listed beneath.

If you tap on the text portion of an Episode listing (for example, Episode 1), it will drop down to show a short description of the episode. On the right, you will notice two icons: an arrow pointing down (which means download) and a play sign (which means stream).

If you tap the play sign, the episode will instantly stream. If you tap the download button, your device will ask you what quality you would like to download (Best, Better, or Good). Tap "Best" for up to 1080p HD, "Better" for 720p HD, or "Good" for SD. "Better" will take the longest and use the most space on your hard drive, while "Good" the least. Normally this will take a little while, but you can let it download in the background and continue to use your device.

Select the "Home" button to go to the Home screen. Now swipe down from the top of your screen to bring up the Quick Settings menu. You will see "Download in progress", with a progress meter and percentage. This is your download! Once it is completed it will be available in your Video Library.

Exploring & Utilizing Your Content Libraries

EBooks Library

Reading Books

To enter your Books Library, select "Books" from the Navigation Bar on the top of your Home screen. Now tap a desired book in your collection. Once the book is open, you can simply swipe left or right in order to flip through the pages. By simply tapping anywhere on the page you will bring up a number of options for reading. At the bottom, you will see a meter with a dot. This tells you your current location, the length of the book, and the percentage of the book you have completed.

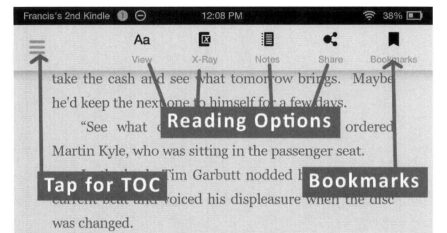

Aa   View   X-Ray   Notes   Share   Bookmarks

Reading Options

Tap for TOC

Bookmarks

take the cash and see what tomorrow brings. Maybe he'd keep the next one to himself for a few days.

"See what ... ordered Martin Kyle, who was sitting in the passenger seat.

In the back, Tim Garbutt nodded his head to the current beat and voiced his displeasure when the disc was changed.

"Aww, I was listening to that."

"Stop bleating, Timmy," Kyle said, switching the CD for something with a bit more drum and bass, "my gran wouldn't even listen to that crap."

Boyle laughed, but his eyes were on the black Skoda coming towards them. The thick aerial first caught his attention, and as it neared he saw the white shirts and black epaulettes of the occupants that identified them as police in an unmarked car. The Skoda passed them and in his rear view mirror he watched it continue for another hundred yards before the blue lights illuminated and it performed a u-turn.

Game on.

Click & Drag to Navigate

* * *

Location 70 of 3398   3%

🏠   ←   🔍

82

You can quickly jump ahead to any part of the book by holding your finger on the dot and sliding to the right. While this isn't extremely precise, it allows you to quickly skip ahead to later chapters and sections. You can hold the dot and slide it back to the left to go back in the book.

Navigating the Table of Contents

You can quickly bring up the Table of Contents from any place in the book, without leaving the text. To do this, tap anywhere on the page. Then tap the icon in the upper left hand corner (the one with 3 parallel lines). You should see a section labeled "Table of Contents" with each chapter listed beneath it. Here you can tap whichever chapter you would like to jump to.

You can also jump to a specific location or page. Again, tap anywhere on the page. Then tap the icon in the upper left hand corner (the one with 3 parallel lines). You should see an option labeled "Go to Page or Location". When you tap this, a pop-up search bar will come up and the keyboard will emerge.

Above the search bar, the device tells you your current location and you can type in a specific location or page, then select either the "Page" or "Location" button, depending on your input. This will bring you to your desired location.

Changing Text Size

Tap anywhere on your book's page. Across the top of your screen, starting from the left side, you will see "View". Tapping this allows you to modify the font, background color, spacing and margins. We'll call this the View Menu. The first two options (from the top down) will increase and decrease the size of your font. Tap the "Aa" icon with the arrow pointing down to decrease the font. Tap as many times as you like to continuously adjust the font.

Changing Background Color

The second row down in the View Menu changes the background color. Tapping the "T" icon all the way to the left changes the background to white. The middle "T" icon gives a Sepia background color (which I find is easiest on the eyes). The "T" icon to the right changes the background color to black (thus changing the text to white).

Changing Margin Size

The third row down in the View Menu changes the size of the margins. The left-side icon makes the margins smaller, allowing for more text. The right-side icon makes the margins larger, meaning less text. The middle icon is a margin size between the two.

Changing Line Spacing

Within the View Menu, the icons in the fourth row down (three parallel line icons) change the space between each line of text. The icon on the left (three lines closest together) condenses the space between the text, while the icon all the way to the right increase the space between the text.

Changing Fonts

In the last row in the View Menu you will see a font name, such as "Georgia". Tap this to bring up a list of fonts, which you can browse by swiping up and down. Tap your desired font.

Using X-Ray While Reading

Tap anywhere on the screen and then tap again to bring the Book Menu back up. To the right of "View", you will see "X-Ray", which will bring up the X-Ray Menu.

X-Ray will give you additional information related to what you are reading. For example, it may give you more details about the location (London, UK), terms, or characters within the text. Across the top, you will see "All", "People", and "Terms". Selecting "People" will give a list of people mentioned in both the current page and the full text, with relevant description pulled from the book. Selecting "Terms" will bring up notable terms, such as places or specific locations.

You can tap on a term to see a full description, supplemented with text passages from the book. This can give you a full understanding of the term. You can also view the Wikipedia page for the term (if applicable) by tapping "Full Wikipedia Article". Tap the arrow in the upper left hand corner to go back. Now, select the "X" in the upper right hand corner to go back to reading view.

Taking Notes While Reading

Within the reading view, tap anywhere on the page. Now select "Notes" within the menu across the top of the screen. This is where your Notes and Marks are stored. We will go over how to write a note and store it. First, select the "X" in the upper right hand corner.

Now select press and hold somewhere on the page. A pop-up menu will appear. Tap "Note" from the menu. A keyboard and text bar will pop-up: here you can type your note. When you are done, select "Save". Your note will be marked and stored!

To access the note you just saved, tap anywhere on the page. Then select "Notes" from the top toolbar. You should see your note listed – tap on it and the device will take you to the page where the note is highlighted.

Adding Bookmarks While Reading

You can add an unlimited number of bookmarks throughout your book in order to hold your place. To add a bookmark, tap anywhere on the page, then tap "Bookmarks" in the upper right hand corner. Tap "Add Bookmark" from the pop-up menu. This will add a bookmark to your current page. If you flip to another page, you can do the same and add another bookmark.

To go to a bookmark, tap anywhere on the page, then tap "Bookmarks". Now tap your desired location from the list of bookmarks (there will be a line of text to indicate the location of your bookmark). You will be brought to the location of the bookmark instantly.

To remove a bookmark, tap anywhere on the page. Then tap "Bookmarks" from the top toolbar. Select the desired bookmark from the list, then tap "Remove Bookmark", located at the top of the pop-up menu (there is a small minus with a circle around it). The bookmark you selected will be removed.

Text-to-Speech For Books

Depending on the publisher, the Kindle Fire HDX has the ability to read text to you. When this text-to-speech is available, you can tap the "Play" button and the content will be read to you.

To change the voice, go to the Home page. Swipe down from the top of the screen to bring down the Quick Settings menu. Select "Settings", then tap "Device". Here, tap "Text-to-Speech". Now you can change the voice by tapping "Default Voice". On most devices, there will be an Australian voice and an American voice (tap the dot to change the default voice).

Tap the arrow in the upper left hand corner to go back. Select "Download Additional Voice" to browse additional voices that are available for download. Tap on a selection to download it. This may take a few moments. Once the download is complete, the voice will be available within the "Default Voice" page.

Taking Out Library Books

With your Kindle Fire HDX, you have the ability to download (essentially "check out"), library books on your Kindle Fire HDX. According to Amazon, there are over 11,000 libraries nationally that let you borrow (check-out) books with your Kindle Fire HDX.

In order to access this service, you will need to download a program named Overdrive. This is a book manager for books that lets you "check-out" books and will automatically delete them from your Kindle when your borrow has expired.

Go to http://search.overdrive.com to download the program.

In order to start downloading books, you will need to check your local library to see if they let you check out eBooks. Normally, you can go to their site and see if this option is listed. You will most likely need a library card, as well as a PIN number (which you need to set-up with them).

Once you are set-up with a library card and a PIN number, you can browse your local library's site for eBooks. Depending on the site, they may have a "Request eBook" feature, which will prompt you for your PIN and Library Card number, while another site may have a "Get for Kindle" option, or something similar. Many have multiple formats for different devices.

Once you successfully select this option, you will be taken to Amazon.com and can check the book out from Amazon's Public

Library Loan page. Select the device you would like the book sent to and then select the "Get library book" option. The book will be delivered to your device.

EBooks From Other Sites

Obviously, Amazon is not the only marketplace for books, though it is the largest. You can download and purchase eBooks from other sources directly on your Kindle Fire HD. Before your purchase, ensure that you are downloading a file that is compatible with your Kindle Fire HDX. Compatible file formats include:

- MOBI
- AZW
- PRC
- KF8 (a new file-type, not frequently used yet)

You can also download books as "Documents" (not "Books"), which you will have to open and read under the "Docs" tab on your top toolbar.

Project Gutenberg

Project Gutenburg is a website and large-scale project which offers digital copies and eBooks of popular and classic public domain books. The site has over 42,000 free books!

Almost all books are available in Kindle format and you can also use a MOBI format on your Kindle Fire HDX. Once you download a book from Project Gutenberg, check "Downloads" within your browser to open the book.

Many of the books available on Project Gutenberg are available for free on Amazon, which is easier than installing the book yourself, as you can just download it immediately to your library.

However, versions may be different on Amazon, as some are abridged and translated for modern-day English.

Newsstand – Magazines & Newspapers

You can read many of your magazine subscriptions directly on your Kindle Fire HDX. The beauty of the device is that it will receive new issues as soon as they are released in the newsstands.

Purchasing Magazines

To find magazines and newspapers, select "Shop" from the Navigation Bar on the Home screen, and then tap "Newsstand". Here, you will see rows of suggested magazine subscriptions, including a rotating carousel at the top, which highlights currently trending magazines. If you swipe up, you will also see sections such as "First 30 Days Free" and "Featured Deals on Kindle Magazines"

If you tap the magnifying glass in the upper right hand corner, you can search for a specific publication.

Magazine & Newspaper Listing Page

Tap a magazine that you would like to take a look at. This will bring you to the magazine listing and description page. Here, you can "Subscribe now" if you are not already a subscriber, by tapping the yellow tab. This will opt you into an Annual subscription. You can also buy individual issues by selecting "Buy Issue", which is located underneath the "Subscribe now" tab. Simply tap the option you would like and your device will begin to download the magazine.

Verifying Subscriptions

If you already have a subscription you can tap "Verify your subscription" in blue text, within the Listing Page. Here, you can choose a few ways to verify your subscription. The easiest way to verify your subscription is to choose the first option and provide your "Account number". Have a paper copy of one of your magazine issues handy and tap the "Subscription account number" box to enter your account number (listed on the magazine). Then tap the "Zip/Postal Code" box and enter your number.

You will then be brought to a page where you will need to create an account by entering a username and password. Once you have done this, the latest issue in your subscription will download to your device.

Quick Tip: Some magazines and newspapers will be available as apps instead of magazines. Usually this is because they have interactive content, including videos and other content. In these cases, when you go to purchase, the Kindle will direct you to the App store, where you can then purchase.

Reading Magazines

Tap "Newsstand" from the Navigation Bar on your Home page. This will bring up a grid of your available magazine issues. Issues you downloaded on previous devices may be listed under the "Cloud" tab located in the upper right hand corner, while issues that are immediately accessible and already downloaded from your device will be listed in both the "Cloud" tab and the "On Device" tab (located in the upper right hand corner).

Note that if you tap the button in the upper left hand corner (3 parallel lines), you can jump to different Newsstand categories within the Amazon Store.

Magazine Navigation

Tap on a magazine to open it. Reading a magazine is much like reading a book. Swipe left and right to flip through the pages. Swipe up and down to scroll up and down on a page (similar to a web page). Tap anywhere on the page to bring up more options across the top and bottom of the screen.

After tapping anywhere on the screen, tap the icon in the upper left hand corner. This will bring up a Table of Contents for the issue. You can swipe up and down on this menu to browse the issues articles. Tap an article title to jump directly to that article.

To go back to reading your magazine, swipe the screen from right to left (where the magazine is still exposed).

You can also browse from a higher-level view of the magazine. Tap anywhere on the page, then tap "Browse" in the upper right hand corner. This will bring you to a high-level view of the issue; swipe right to left to quickly scroll through the issue. Tap the lower portion of the screen to exit.

Bookmarking Magazines

Much like books, you can place bookmarks within magazines that you are reading. From the reading view, tap anywhere on the page. Then tap Bookmarks. Here you can add, delete, and jump to bookmarks. This works exactly the same as bookmarking within books.

Music

The Kindle Fire HDX is a great device for listening to music, as it is equipped with Dolby Digital Plus. Whether listening through headphones, a stereo, or with the device's built-in speaker, the HDX provides a cutting-edge listening experience.

Dolby Digital Plus is able to optimize the device's sound depending on your listening circumstances. This means it can create virtual surround sound, adjust volume automatically, and allow for easier listening of dialogue.

Shopping for Music on Amazon

To shop for music on Amazon, tap "Shop" from the toolbar across the top of the Home screen, then select "Music". This will bring you to the Amazon Music Store.

Across the top of the screen will be a rotating carousel of deals and advertisements for various artists and genres. Below that will be a list of Bestselling Songs and Albums. Scroll through these categories by swiping left and right. View more featured categories by swiping up to scroll down.

From this screen you can tap the magnifying glass icon in the upper right hand corner to search for a specific song, album, or artist. A keyboard will pop-up and you can type in your selection, or tap "Cancel" to go back.

From the main Music Store menu, tap the icon on the upper left hand side (3 parallel lines). About halfway down the Navigation Panel you should see "Shop". Under this will be a few categories that you can jump to, including "Best Sellers", "New Releases", "Browse Genres" and "Gift Cards & Promotions".

Purchasing Music

To purchase an album, tap on the album's icon within the Music Store. You will be brought to the album's listing page. Here, you can purchase the entire album by tapping the yellow "Buy Album" near the top of the listing. Below this, you should see a full track list for the album.

You can purchase individual songs by tapping the smaller yellow boxes next to the songs. Within the boxes is the price per song. To preview the song, tap the "Play" button to the left of the song title. This will sample a portion of the song.

Quick Tip: Usually the full album is more cost effective than purchasing each song, so look to take advantage of this if you are a fan of the album or artist.

Swipe down on the album listing page to view "Customers Also Bought" suggestions as well as customer reviews, and an "About the Artist" page.

Music Store Settings

In the main Music Store page, tap the upper left hand icon (3 parallel lines), then tap "Settings". Here, you can choose to toggle "Automatic Downloads" On/Off (this will automatically download any purchase to your device). You can also clear your cached songs by tapping "Clear Cache". This may free up a bit of space on your storage drive.

Adding Your Own Music

You can easily add your own music to your Kindle Fire HDX. First, use the USB cable that came with the device to hook-up your HDX to your computer.

Mac users will need to download an "Android File Transfer" application on their computer. Go to Kindle.com/support/downloads to follow the directions and download this. Once you download and install this, you are ready to transfer files.

Windows XP users will need to install the latest version of Windows Media Player in order to transfer files.

If you are using a PC, your USB storage will be mounted as a drive and appear in your Computer or My Computer folder. You can drag files from your PC into this drive, just as you would any other drive. Once you are finished, eject the device from your Windows file browser before unplugging.

If you are using a Mac, open your "Android File Transfer" program on your computer. Here, you will see a series of folders. These are folders within your Kindle Fire HDX.

Locate the album or music files on your Mac that you would like to transfer. Now drag these files or folders into the "Music" folder within the Android File Transfer program. Depending on the file sizes, they may take anywhere from a few seconds to nearly an hour (if you are uploading say your entire music collection).

To disconnect your Kindle, open a file manager and select "Eject Android File Transfer". You are now free to disconnect the device from your computer.

Once the transfer is complete, this music will now be available to listen to on your HDX. Select "Music" from the Home screen on your device. Now select "On Device" in the upper right hand corner. Your music should be available.

Playlists

Building playlists on the Kindle Fire HDX allows you to arrange a selection of songs, from any of your albums, to play consecutively. The Kindle Fire HDX makes building playlists very easy.

Building a Playlist

To make a new playlist, go to your Music Library. Now tap the icon on the upper left hand corner (3 parallel lines) and select "Playlists". Note: if you are in the "Cloud" section, you can only see music that is on your cloud and if you are in the "On Device" section you can only see music that is on your device locally.

To create a new playlist, tap the "+" sign in the upper right hand corner of your screen. You will be asked to name your playlist. Type in a name using the keyboard and tap "Save".

Note: If you create the playlist on the "Cloud", you can only use tracks on the cloud and if you create the playlist "On Device", you can only use tracks on your device locally. Be mindful of which one you create your playlist in.

Once you enter your playlist name, you will be taken to a screen where you can add tracks to your playlist. You can browse tracks by Playlists, Artists, Albums, Songs, or Genres, from left to right across the top of your screen. To add a track, tap the yellow "+" sign to the right of the track's length. You can remove the track by selecting the "-" icon. You can browse through all your tracks here and create your playlist.

When you are happy with your playlist, select "Done" in the upper right hand corner. You can always add tracks to your playlist later on. You will now be able to play your playlist.

Playing Your Playlist

Tap "Play All" to begin playback. This will take you to the current track, where you can pause, skip, or go back a track. You can also shuffle tracks from this view. Tap the arrow in the upper left hand side to go back to your playlist.

Adding Songs & Deleting Playlists

While you are browsing your tracks from your Music Library, you can easily add tracks to your playlists on the fly. Simply press and hold on an album or track. A pop-up menu will appear; select "Add to playlist". This will bring up a list of your playlists; tap the desired playlist and your song will be added to that playlist.

To delete a playlists, go to the "Playlists" section of your Music Library. Now, press and hold on the desired playlist. Select "Remove from Device". This will merely delete the playlist, not the songs from the device.

Audiobooks

You can easily listen to audiobooks on your Kindle Fire HDX. To purchase audiobooks, select "Shop" from the main menu on the home screen, then select "Audiobooks". This is the Audiobooks Store; you can browse through suggestions on the storefront or search for a specific book. You will notice beneath each book is a "Play Sample" option. Tapping this will start a 5-minute audio sample from the book. Press the button again to stop the playback.

Purchasing Audiobooks

To purchase, tap on the cover of an audiobook. You will be brought to the listing page for your selected audiobook. Tap the "Buy" button underneath the "Get this Free" button. You may need to enter your credit card information if you do not have an Audible.com account.

Listening to Audiobooks

Once you have completed downloading an audiobook, you can select "Listen Now" to open up and start the audiobook. You will see a few options across the bottom. Starting from the bottom left, you can go back in 30 seconds increments, pause the audiobook, or insert a bookmark. (You can also long-press to insert a note).

With the icons located on the bottom right hand side (from left to right) you can set up a sleep timer, adjust the narration speed, or adjust the volume. If you tap the icon in the upper right hand corner (3 parallel lines) you can view a clickable Table of Contents. Tap a chapter to jump the playback to that chapter. In the upper right hand corner, you can view your bookmarks. Tap a bookmark to jump to that spot.

Audiobook Library

To access your Audiobook Library, select "Audiobooks" from the top menu on the Home screen. Here, you will see a grid style layout of your audiobooks on your cloud and on your device locally.

Whispersync

If you purchase both the audiobook and eBook versions of a book, Amazon's "Whispersync" service will automatically sync the two versions for you. You can see whether or not a book is supported by Whispersync by checking for "Whispersync for Voice" on the book's listing page.

Audible

Audible is an audiobook service owned by Amazon, which integrates seamlessly with your Kindle Fire HDX. Amazon will automatically create an account for you when you purchase an audiobook via Amazon. You can log in at Audible.com using your same username and password.

Apps & Games

The Kindle Fire HDX has tons of popular apps and best-selling games, many of which are free to download. To access Amazon's vast App store, tap "Shop" in the upper left hand corner of the Home screen, then tap "Apps" on the right hand side. This is the App Store. You will see a number of categories within the App Store, such as "Featured Apps and Games" and "Recommend For You Based on Your Book Interests". You can browse these categories by swiping up and down.

You will also see a carousel-style banner across the top that features advertisements for various apps and categories (including "Today's Free App of the Day"). Tap on these ads to jump to the relevant app, game or category.

From the main app store screen, you can scroll Apps within categories by swiping right to left. (For example, under "Featured Apps and Games", swipe to the left to view more apps within that category). You can also tap the magnifying glass icon in the upper right hand side to search for a specific app.

Downloading & Purchasing Apps

Tap on an App's icon in order to go to the listing for that app. In the listing, you will see a yellow bar with the price in dollars ($0.99) or the price in coins (99 coins). We'll talk more about Amazon Coins next. You will also see a series of yellow stars followed by a number. This is the App's user rating, based on ratings & reviews submitted by those who downloaded and used the app (the number is how many rating the App has). You can use this to make educated decisions on how well the app will function.

Below the yellow purchase bar, you will see "Screenshots". Here you can swipe right to left to view various screenshots of the app. Tap the screenshot to expand it. From this expanded view, you can continue to browse screenshots by swiping left and right. When you want to exit the Screenshot viewer and go back to the listing, simply tap on the screenshot once more to go back.

Below this you will see "Description"; this is a blurb that gives you a brief description of the app, as well as "Key Details" on the right hand side. Scrolling down more will give you recommendations based on those who purchased this app and you will also see the "Customer Reviews" section, which shows the reviews deemed "Most Helpful".

Once you are satisfied with the app's details, scroll back up to purchase the app. If the app is free, it will download once you tap the yellow bar that says "Free", then tap "Get App". Now the app will be downloaded. When it is completed, you can open it by tapping "Open" right on the listing page.

If the app is paid, you will need to tap the yellow bar that states the app's price. This will bring you to another window, which asks if you want to buy the app with Amazon Coins or money. To pay with the credit card attached to your Amazon account, simply make sure the dot to the right of the US dollar option is highlighted. Then, tap "Get App" to make your purchase. The app will now be available in your App Library.

Amazon Coins

Amazon Coins are a new way to purchase apps and games for the Kindle Fire HDX. You can purchase coins directly from Amazon, then spend them on the Amazon marketplace. These coins can be used for apps, games, as well as in-app items. There is no expiration date for the coins and there are no added fees. Amazon Coins give you the opportunity to save money when you use them for purchases.

For a point of reference, 100 Amazon Coins = $1.00. You can purchase the coins in 5 denominations: 500, 1000, 2500, 5000,

10000 and you will get a better deal the higher denomination you purchase. For example, 500 Amazon Coins costs $4.80 (a 4% savings), while 10,000 costs $90.00 (a 10% savings).

Note: Every Kindle Fire user is given 500 free coins to use, so you can try these out before you ever decide to purchase more. They will be preloaded with your device once you link it with your Amazon account.

To use the coins, simply make sure the Amazon Coins option is highlighted in the check-out screen (after tapping the yellow bar to purchase the app).

Test Driving Apps

In the app's listing, you will see a small green bar under the app's icon, which gives you the option to "Test Drive" the app. Tapping this will open the app in a window and will let you use the app for a few minutes.

This allows you to make more educated decisions when you are looking to purchase apps and, for the most part, this will give you full-use of the app. You will see a small timer in the upper left hand corner that is counting down; this is how much time you have left to test-drive the app.

Once you are satisfied, you can tap "Quit" in upper left hand corner to finish testing the app. You can also choose to purchase by tapping the yellow tab with the price in the upper right hand corner.

Purchasing Games

Downloading and purchasing games is much the same as downloading apps. To access the Games store, tap "Shop" in the upper left hand corner of the Home screen, then tap "Games".

This is the Game store; it has the same layout as the App store and similar style listings. You can purchase Games within the Games store and (similar to Apps) can also use Amazon Coins to purchase.

GameCircle

Amazon GameCircle allows you to automatically keep your progress in games. This service will save all your scores, achievements, and high scores and allows you to compete on global Leaderboards. Games will need to be GameCircle enabled in order to take advantage of this service.

Photos & Video

The Kindle Fire HDX is great for viewing and storing both photos and video. The high-resolution screen allows your media to shine and the interface is very intuitive for browsing photos.

Browsing Photos

To browse photos, tap "Photos" from the Navigation Bar on the upper right hand side of the Home screen. This will bring you to a grid style view of all photos that you have uploaded to the device, as well as photos and video you have taken with the camera. To view a photo, simply tap on the desired photo.

Here, you can tap anywhere on the photo and you will have 3 options across the upper right hand side of the screen. You can jump to the camera; share your photo to social media (with three dots connect by lines), and edit/delete photos (with the 3 vertical dots icon). Tap the arrow in the upper left hand corner to go back to the "All" photos view.

Posting Photos to Social Media Networks

The icon with three dots connect by lines, is the "Share" button. Tap this to share this picture via Email, Facebook, or Twitter. If you have not yet set-up Facebook, Twitter, or Email on your HDX you will be prompted to go to your settings to enter your account information. Tap "Go to Settings" to view your Social Network Accounts page. Tap "Facebook". Here you can enter your username and password using the on-screen keyboard. When you are done, tap "Connect" and your account will be linked. You can now post photos to Facebook.

Sharing Multiple Photos

To share multiple photos to social media, first make sure you are in the "All" photos view, which shows a grid of all your photos. Now select the icon in the upper right hand corner with 3 dots connected by lines. Now, you can tap multiple photos to share. Tap the ones you would like, then tap your desired social media network from the top of the screen.

Editing & Deleting Photos

Once you have snapped a picture, the Kindle Fire HDX has a ton of options to edit your photo. You can adjust everything from Contrast and Saturation, to applying stickers, inserting text, and turning your picture into a meme-style photo.
While browsing your photos within the Camera app, tap anywhere to bring up a toolbar across the top. The icon with 3 vertical dots in the upper right hand corner allows you to Delete, Edit, or view Info on this photo. Tap "Delete" to remove the current photo from the device.

Tapping "Edit" will allow you to customize the photo. Here, you can access a plethora of settings: Enhance, Crop, Rotate, Redeye, Filters, Stickers, Text, Meme, Draw, Brightness, Contrast, Saturation, Warmth, Whiten, Blemish, Sharpness, Focus, Splash. Tap "Filters" to apply Instagram-style filters to your photo. When you are done, select "Done". A new picture will be added with your edits.

While viewing a photo, tap anywhere on the screen, then tap the arrow in the upper left hand corner of the screen to view your Camera Roll. This will show you a grid-style view of all your photos, which you can use to quickly browse.

Transferring Photos & Video

To transfer photos and video, connect your Kindle Fire HDX to your computer via the USB cable that came in your box.

Mac users - Note: if you have not done so already, you will have to download the "Android File Transfer" application on your computer. Visit http://kindle.com/support/downloads and follow the instruction here to download the file to your computer. Once the "Android File Transfer" is installed on your computer, you are ready to transfer files.

Windows XP users will need to install the latest version of Windows Media Player in order to transfer files.

Once you are ready to go, the Android File Transfer folder will automatically pop-up on your computer. (If you are using a PC, the drive will be automatically mounted as a USB Storage Drive, located in Computer or My Computer). You will see a number of folders, including Books, Documents, Movies, Music, etc. Drag the desired file(s) from your computer to the corresponding folder in the directory. For example, if you would like to transfer a movie or video, drag this file into "Movies". If you would like to transfer a photo, drag them into "Pictures". Once you are done, eject your device from your computer. You can now view your uploaded content in the "Videos Library" or "Photos Library".

Quick Tip: Videos you add may be located in your "Photos" library, as they may not be recognized as movies or TV Shows.

Note: You must ensure you have the correct file format for your content, or else it will not work on your Kindle.

For video, the Kindle Fire HDX supports:
MP4, 3GP, VP8 (with video playback at 720p)

For photos, the Kindle Fire HDX supports:
JPEG, GIF, PNG, BMP

For audio, the Kindle Fire HDX supports:

E-AC-3 (Dolby Digital Plus), AC-3 (Dolby Digital), MP3, AAC (.m4a), OGG, MIDI, MP4, WAV, AAC LC/LTP, HE-AACv2, HE-AACv1, AMR-WB, AMR, NB

For documents, the Kindle Fire HDX supports:
AZW, PDF, TXT, PRC, DOCX, DOC

Streaming Video from Other Sites

You can stream video, including movies and TV shows, from sites other than Amazon. For example, Netflix and Hulu (very popular streaming video sites) offer their apps for free on the Amazon store. Simply download the app from the Apps store and enter your account information (if you already have an account). You will be able to watch Netflix and Hulu streaming movies and shows right from your HDX!

YouTube

Currently, there is no YouTube app on the Kindle Store. However, if you open your browser and go to www.youtube.com, you will automatically be directed to the mobile version of the site, which will allow you to play video. This works very well and you can even play videos in HD, if the video supports it.

Documents

Tap "Docs" in the Navigation Bar on the Home screen to enter your Documents Library. Here, you can choose to add Docs to your library in 4 ways: Email, Sync, Clip, and Transfer.

Transferring Docs

The easiest way is transferring files from your computer to your Kindle Fire HDX. Simply attach your computer and HDX with the USB cable and open Android File Transfer on Mac, or your Windows file browser on PC. You will see a folder called "Documents". Simply drag and drop the desired document into this folder and it will be available on your device. Eject your Kindle and disconnect the USB cable when you are completed.

Note: Your transferred document will be available in the "On Device" tab within your Documents Library, as it is on the device locally and not on the Cloud.

You can easily email documents to your Kindle. Simply send your documents to the Kindle email address given to you (or the account you have linked with your Email app) and they will be available in your Documents Library. To find your email address, tap the "Email" icon within the Documents Library.

Syncing Docs with Amazon Cloud

You can also sync docs with your Amazon Cloud drive by tapping "Sync", then tapping "Email me install links". This will automatically send you a link to download the Amazon Cloud Drive desktop app. Once you have installed this App, any document you add to the Amazon Cloud Drive will be available on your Kindle Fire HDX.

Send-to-Kindle (Clip Articles)

You can install the Send-to-Kindle button on your PC or Mac to quickly and seamlessly send articles, blog posts, and other content to read on your Kindle. To install Send-to-Kindle, tap the "Clip" icon within the Docs Library. Now, tap "Email me install links"; the link to install Send-to-Kindle will be emailed to your registered email address.

Once Send-to-Kindle is installed on your browser, you select the correct device to send articles to. Once this is set, you can send articles to your device with the click of a button. You should see the "K" icon in the toolbar on your browser. It will take a few minutes for the article to be formatted and sent.

Reading & Editing Documents

Reading Kindle documents (articles that you send to your device) is almost exactly the same as books. Swipe left or right to turn pages. By tapping anywhere on the page, you bring up a few options, such as changing the format, as well as adding notes and bookmarks. You can also slide the dot at the bottom of the screen left or right to quickly jump through the document.

You can also read and edit .Doc/.Docx files. In the Documents Library, open a .doc file by tapping on it. Here, you can swipe up and down and left to right to browse the document. To zoom in and out, "pinch" the screen with two fingers (it's easiest with your thumb and index finger). Draw your fingers closer to zoom out, and further away to zoom in.

In order to edit your document, you will need to install "OfficeSuite Pro", which is normally $14.99. Once you have installed this, tap "Edit" on the top toolbar of your document to begin editing.

To search your .doc document, tap the "Find" icon in the upper right hand corner. Here, you can enter text you would like to search for, then use the left and right arrows to the right of the text to flip through locations where the text is found. Tap "Done" to close the finder.

Printing Documents

You can also choose to print your documents. Across the top of the screen there will be a "Print" button; tap this to search for printers. Your device will automatically convert your doc to a PDF, then search the network for printers. You can print wirelessly, however your printer will need to support wireless printing and you may need to download an app on your Kindle (for example, an HP app for an HP printer). You can also easily email the document to your PC or Mac and print from there.

Browsing the Internet

As discussed in the Quick Start Guide portion of this user manual, the Kindle Fire HDX comes loaded with Amazon's stock browser, Silk. Silk is a fast, dependable browser with easy-to-use features.

To open Silk, swipe up from the bottom of your Home screen to bring up the Grid View, then select tap on the Silk icon. Silk opens with a new tab and a list of your most visited sites, of which you can tap to go to.

Silk features tabbed browsing. To open a new tab, simply tap the "+" sign in the upper right hand corner. This allows you to browse multiple sites within the same browser. Tap on your open tabs to switch between different tabs. To close a tab, tap the small (x) on the right hand side of the tab.

Full Screen Mode & Navigation

Once you visit a website, you will have a number of options available at the bottom of your screen. You will see square-shaped icon with four arrows pointing in 4 different directions. Tapping this icon opens full-screen mode: your current webpage will take up the entire screen. To exit full-screen mode, swipe up from the small tab at the bottom of the screen.

While you are on a website, tap the icon with the parallel lines and a box around them (to the left of the magnifying glass). This will bring up the Navigation Panel on the left, with a few different options. You can share this page via Email, Twitter or Facebook. You can also "Request Another View"; this means you can choose to open the page as a mobile page or a desktop page. This may be good if the mobile page is not operating properly or it is missing contents.

Tap the icon in the upper left hand corner (3 parallel lines). Here, you can view your Most Visited sites, jump to your Bookmarks, Downloads, or History. Tapping "History" will show your latest visited sites, in order of the dates you visited them. There is a tab for "Today", as well as "Yesterday" and the "Last 7 days". Tap "Today" to collapse the list, and tap again to expand.

Bookmarking a Webpage

To bookmark a website, first go to that website in an open tab. Then press and hold the tab until a pop-up menu appears. Tap "Add to Bookmarks". Now you can edit the name and location – make sure you leave the location as-is. Tap "OK" when you are done and this page will be added to your bookmarks.

To view all your bookmarks, tap the icon in the upper left hand corner (3 parallel lines), then tap "Bookmarks". You will see a grid-style layout with your bookmarks. By tapping "Bookmarks" near the upper left hand corner of the screen, you can choose to sort by Last Accessed, Title, or Number of Visits. You can also change the layout to a list: tap the icon with 4 small parallel vertical lines in the upper right hand corner (next to the 4 squares icon). This will display your bookmarks in a list.

You can also add bookmarks from the Bookmarks manager. Tap "Add" in the upper right hand corner to add a bookmark manually. You will need to enter the Name and Title, then tap "OK".

Tapping once on the bookmark will open it in the browser. If you press and hold on the bookmark, you will be able to open the bookmark in a new tab, share the bookmark, copy the URL, or edit/delete the bookmark.

Sharing Bookmarks

To share a bookmark, press and hold on the desired bookmark. Then tap "Share Link". You can share this link via Email, or to your Twitter or Facebook accounts. Once your accounts are linked, this is seamless. Tapping "Email" will bring up a new email message containing the link, which you can easily send to a recipient.

Trending Now

Tapping "Trending Now" on the sidebar will bring you to a page with various news articles that are currently trending and popular. These are mainly from large news sources, such as CNN, NY Times, and Yahoo. Tap the boxes in the upper right hand corner to toggle between list view and grid view.

Browser Settings

To access your browser settings, tap the icon on the upper left hand side to bring up the sidebar, then tap "Settings". The first setting you can change is the default Search Engine used when you type in a search term. Tap "Search Engine"; then select either Bing, Google, or Yahoo. These are the 3 search engine options.

The Next setting is Block Pop-Up Windows. You can choose to always block pop-ups, never block pop-ups, or be asked if you want Silk to block a pop-up. The default setting is "Ask", which means Silk will prompt you when a pop-up comes up.

You can also toggle "Accelerate Page Loading", "Optional Encryption", and "Enable Instant Page Loads". We suggest that you leave these as is, as this will optimize your browsing speeds.

From the settings, you can clear your history and your cache (this included cached content from webpages). You can toggle Cookies On/Off and clear your cookies. You can also have your

Kindle remember passwords that you enter for websites (toggling this on may be helpful). You can also clear passwords and choose whether or not to remember form data (to automatically fill in forms later on).

You can also enable your location, so geo-location websites can provide you with relevant content. "Individual Website Data" shows you data on specific sites you have visited. You can also choose whether or not you would like Silk to prompt you before beginning a download. This is highly recommended, so you do not download a malicious file accidently.

You can also edit some "Advanced" settings. You can stop your browser from loading images (perhaps if you have a slow connection), as well as choose to disable JavaScript, disable security warnings, and disable streaming viewer (an experimental media viewer for eligible content). Lastly, you can reset all your default settings.

Camera

The Kindle Fire HDX 7-inch has a front-facing camera, while the Kindle Fire HDX 8.9-inch has a both a front and rear facing camera. At the current time, the Kindle Fire HDX 8.9 is not available for purchase, so we will cover the Kindle Fire HDX 7-inch.

Taking Pictures with the Camera

To open the Camera, swipe up on the Home screen to open the Grid View. Tap the "Camera" icon. The screen will now show the camera view. Tap the circular icon in the middle of the bottom of the screen to snap a picture.

To view the photo, tap the icon on the bottom right (which should show the picture you just snapped). You can browse through the photos you have taken by swiping left or right.

Shooting Video with the Camera

With the camera open, tap the icon on the upper left hand side of the screen. This will switch your camera to a video camera. Tap the red button at the bottom of the screen to start recording, and tap it again when you are done. You can view your video by tapping on the icon in the bottom right hand corner of the screen. There should be a screenshot of you video. To play, just tap the screen when the photo from your video is on the screen.

Quick Tip: Video shot with the Camera will be stored within the Photo Library, not the Video Library.

Browsing Photos You Have Taken with the Camera

To browse photos you have taken with the camera, go to the camera. Then tap the icon in the bottom right hand side of the screen (should be a small screenshot of your latest photo taken). Here, you can swipe back and forth to browse photos.

Tap anywhere on the photo to bring up a toolbar across the top of the screen. Here you will see three icons across the upper right hand side of the screen. The first one from the left, the camera icon, will bring you back to the live camera. Tap it and you will be able to take a photo.

Rear-Facing HD Camera (Kindle Fire HDX 8.9")

The Kindle Fire HDX 8.9 will come equipped with a high-definition rear-facing camera. This camera comes equipped with an LED flash and can shoot HDR images, 1080p video as well as support for panoramic images and "burst" images. The photo app includes numerous photo-editing features that you can use on images you take.

Productivity

Setting Up Your Email

From the Home screen, tap "Apps", then tap "Email". You will be prompted to enter your email address. If you are using Gmail, you will be taken to a Google page where you will be prompted to enter your Gmail account password. Once you are done, you will be able to access your email via the Email app. You can now click "Go to Your Inbox" to view your email.

Also, from the Apps Library, you will notice a small number on the bottom left hand corner of the Email app – these are your new emails.

Note: Kindle supports Gmail, Hotmail, Yahoo Mail, and AOL. It also supports POP and IMAP email set-ups.

Using Email

Once your email is set-up, open your Email App. You will see a list of your latest emails. Bolded emails are emails that you haven't opened yet. You can swipe up and down on the screen to browse emails (the latest will be on the top). From the main Inbox view, you have a few options, including composing an email and viewing your folders.

Sending an Email

To compose a new message, tap the icon in the upper right hand corner titled "New". This will bring you to a new screen with an email form. Here, you can type in the recipients email, the subject, Cc/Bcc others, or change which address the email will send from. (Note: you must have multiple email accounts set-up to do this).

If you tap the white space beneath the "Subject" field, you can start composing your message. In the upper right hand corner, tap the icon with 3 vertical dots. This will bring up a pop-up menu. Here you can attach photos, files, show formatting, save a draft, or discard the message.

Tap "Show Formatting" to bring up a formatting toolbar within your email. This is very helpful for quickly formatting text within an email. You can adjust size, choose bold, italics, and underline, as well as a select font and highlight color. When you are done, tap "Send" in the upper right hand corner to send your email.

Viewing Email Folders

To view your folders, tap the icon with 3 parallel lines in the upper left hand corner. You will see your "Inbox", as well as an "Unread" folder. Tap "Show labels" to view all your separate folders. Here, you can jump to folders such as your Outbox, Sent mail, Drafts, or Junk. This is helpful for finding emails you sent or ones that went to your Junk folder. Tap the back button on the bottom of the screen to go back to your Inbox.

Email Settings

From the main Email view, tap the icon with 3 parallel lines, in the upper left hand corner. Tap "Settings", then tap "Email General Settings". Here, you can adjust default message text size, choose to show embedded images, automatically download attachments, choose to include original message in replies, show conversations, and auto-advance.

Gmail Settings

You can also edit your Gmail Settings from your Kindle Fire HDX. From the main email view, tap the upper left hand corner icon (3 parallel lines), then tap Settings. Towards the bottom, you should see "Gmail"; select this. Here, you can edit your Gmail account, including your name and account description. You can also choose whether you want to sync email, calendar and contacts, as well as select your inbox check frequency, how long you store messages, and create a signature for your emails.

Contacts

Contacts will automatically be synced from your email account. When you begin to type in an email recipient in a new message, the Email client will automatically give you relevant contact suggestions. To access a list of your contacts, go to the Home page. Within the carousel (that swipes left to right), locate your Calendar or Email app.

Beneath either of these, you will see 3 icons: the star icon to the right is the VIP/Contacts list. Select this; you will be brought to your VIP list. If you tap the icon in the upper right hand corner (3 parallel lines), you will see an "All Contacts" category. Tap this to view all your contacts.

Contact Settings

From the contact folder, tap the icon in the upper right hand corner (3 parallel lines). Tap "Settings", then tap "Contacts General Settings". Here, you can choose to back up your Amazon contacts on the cloud or delete them from the cloud, as well as sort the order of your contacts and how their name will be displayed.

Adding a Contact

To manually add a contact, go to an email sent from that person. Press and hold on their photo/icon in the upper left hand corner (next to their email). Here you can select "Add to Contacts". You will be brought to a form with their contact information. You can add more information, such as their phone and address. Tap "Save" in the upper right hand corner when you are done.

VIP's

VIP's are simply important contacts that you can add to keep track of emails from them. To view your VIP folder, open your Email app. Tap the 3 parallel lines icon in the upper left hand corner, then select "VIP". This will show all emails from your VIP contacts. Note: this will only show emails dating from when you added them to your VIP list.

To add a VIP contact, tap their icon/photo within an email. If you have already added them as a contact, a small box will pop up with their email address. Tap the star in the upper right hand corner. The star will turn yellow. Now this contact is added to your VIP list.

Calendar

To access your calendar, tap "Apps" on the Navigation Bar in the Home screen, then tap "Calendar". The beauty of the calendar app on the Kindle Fire HDX is that it is automatically syncs with your Gmail account (if you set one up with email). Your appointments and events will be automatically uploaded and viewable in the Calendar.

Changing Calendar View

By default, the Calendar will be open in Weekly view. Swipe left or right to go forward or back a week. Tap "Today" in the upper right hand corner to jump to the current day. To leave weekly view, tap the icon that reads "Calendar" in the upper left hand corner (you should see "Week" under it). Here, you can select Day, Week, Month, or List.

Selecting "Day" will give you a granular overview of the current day, hour by hour. Swipe left or right to go back or forward a day. Selecting "List" will show a list of all your appointments (both upcoming and past) with the date and time of each.

Adding Events

To add an appointment/event, tap the 3 vertical dots in the upper right hand corner, then tap "New Event". Here, you can enter the Title of your event, the Location, and when the event starts and ends. You can also have the event repeat, add reminders, and invite contacts.

Once you have filled in all desired information, tap "Save" in the upper right hand corner to save the event. If you are using Gmail, this event will also automatically be added to your Google Calendar.

Calendar Settings

To edit your Calendar Settings, tap the icon in the upper left hand corner (3 parallel lines). Tap "Settings", then tap "Calendar General Settings". Here, you will see 4 options: "Set Reminder Time", "Week Starts On", "Use Default Time Zone", and "Set Default Time Zone".

Battery Life Best Practices

Displaying Exact Percentage of Battery Remaining

In the status bar the battery indicator will be shown by default; this will give you an estimate of how much power remains. To display the exact percentage remaining, enter the Quick Settings screen by swiping down on the screen.

Tap on settings, and then tap on Device, to display the Show Battery Percentage option. Toggle this setting on and a percentage of your remaining battery will now be shown next to the battery icon in your status bar.

Conserving Battery

Your Kindle HDX has an expected battery life of up to 11 hours (or 17 hours if you are just reading), but this varies greatly depending on how you use your device.

To maximize the battery life of your HDX, you may choose to adjust the following settings/features:

Notifications
By disabling notification alerts you can increase battery life. Enabling Quiet Time by tapping the Quiet Time icon found with your Quick Settings will stop all notifications.

You can also individually disable notifications for your apps and utilities by visiting the Notifications & Quiet Time settings found on your Settings Screen. Just tap on each individual application to bring up their notifications. Toggle the On/Off button to disable notifications.

Brightness
Access your Quick Settings screen once again and tap on Brightness. Lowering your screen's brighten will help conserve battery.

Wireless
Turning off your wireless will save life battery as well. In Quick Settings, tap the wireless icon and then toggle Airplane Mode on. This will disable your Wireless connectivity.

Headphones
Using headphones when you listen to audio will conserve battery life whereas using the external speakers will drain battery life quicker. Plug your headphones into the headphones jack found right next to the volume buttons on the rear side of the device.

Sleep Mode
You can increase battery life by adjusting your screen to enter sleep mode more quickly. Access your Quick Settings screen by swiping down from the top of your device. Tap on settings, and then tap on Display & Sounds. From here, tap the Display Sleep

button. Reduce the time it takes for your HDX to enter sleep mode to save battery life when you're not using it.

Email
You can set the frequency for which your HDX checks for new emails. Swipe down to enter your quick settings page and then tap on settings. From the settings page, tap on applications. From within applications, tap on the email, contacts, and calendar button. Find the email account you wish to select and tap inbox check frequency. From here, reduce the frequency for which your Inbox is checked for new messages.

Security

The Kindle Fire HDX has a number built-in security options that you can use for added reassurance. However, one of the most important features is that the device makes 1-Click purchases; this means that your credit card number and information are not sent across the network each time you make a purchase.

Wi-Fi Security

The first security option you will come across is when you connect to your Wi-Fi network. Your Kindle Fire HDX will automatically detect what kind of security your Wi-Fi connection is using and match it appropriately. The Kindle Fire HDX supports Wired Equivalent Privacy (WEP), Wi-Fi Protected Access (WPA), and MAC Filtering (Media Access Control). WEP and WPA both simply require you to enter passwords to connect.

MAC Filtering

Some networks only allow specific devices to connect; they do this by checking the device's MAC address to decide if the device is safe. If your network is filtering MAC addresses, you may need to add your device's MAC address to your router's settings.

To locate your MAC address, swipe down from the top of the screen to bring up the Quick Settings menu, and then tap Wireless. You should see your device's MAC Address listed here.

Password Protecting Your Device

If you are worried about other's gaining access to your device, you can add a password in order for the device to be unlocked. To add a password, swipe down from the top of the Home screen to bring up the Quick Settings. Now select "Settings", then tap

"Security". Here you will see "Lock Screen Password". Toggle the meter on the right to "On" and you will be able to enter a PIN number (at least 4 numbers).

After you have entered a PIN, anyone who tries to use your device will have to enter a password at the lock screen.

Location-Based Services Security

Location-Based Services allow 3rd party apps and website to gather location data on your device. This can then be used for app functionality (for example, using MapQuest) or marketing purposes (location-based ads, etc.). The Kindle Fire HDX allows you to toggle Location-Based Services on or off.

To access Location-Based Services, swipe down from the top of the Home screen, then tap "Settings", and then "Wireless". Here you will see "Location-Based Services"; tap the bar to the right of this to toggle this setting "On" or "Off".

Note: When you turn Location-Based Services on, you will need to approve the use of this by tapping "Continue". Now your apps and websites you visit will be able to use location data on your device.

Advanced Features

MayDay

Mayday is Amazon's new customer service feature that is available to help users navigate their device. Since Amazon's marketplace is highly integrated into it's tablet devices, this feature is intended to help guide the user experience, assist in the buying experience, and act as an overall help center.

Tapping the Mayday button from your quick settings screen will take you to the Amazon Assist main screen, containing the Mayday feature.

To enable Mayday, tap the yellow connect button and you will be connected to an Amazon tech advisor. You will be connected within 15 seconds (as noted by Amazon). This advisor will be able to see what your screen is displaying, but will not see you nor your account information. You will be able to see advisor live on your HDX screen. This advisor will guide you through any feature on your HDX and can even draw on the screen. They will walk you through step-by-step on how to do something or even do it for you.

Mayday assistance is available at all times, 24/7/365, and is absolutely free for U.S. customers. Currently, there are only English speaking agents on call. Mayday works best when there's a strong Wi-Fi connection.

4G Technology

Your Kindle HDX supports 4G LTE technology, allowing you to operate your device on-the-go at the speed of Wi-Fi. AT&T and Verizon both offer data plan options to support your HDX device is you wish to activate this 4G technology.

Here are the links to the proper data plan offerings:
ATT - http://www.att.com/shop/wireless/plans-new.html#fbid=7K2ASUJ66FA
Verizon -
http://www.verizonwireless.com/wcms/consumer/shop/share-everything.html

How to connect to 4G:
http://www.amazon.com/gp/help/customer/display.html/ref=help_search_1-1?ie=UTF8&nodeId=201176350&qid=1382670989&sr=1-1

http://www.amazon.com/gp/help/customer/display.html?nodeId=201239840

Kindle Free Time

Amazon's new feature, Kindle Free Time, was designed for HDX users whose device will be shared with children. Kindle Free time is a standalone app that comes preloaded on your device and found on the home screen. This app allows the device owner to create separate user profiles for children. Amazon suggests these profiles be created for children ages 3 to 8, but you can use this app in whatever manner you prefer.

Kindle FreeTime allows you to assign access to all of your content on an individual or categorical basis to the user profiles you create. For example, you may wish to create a profile for your 5 year old daughter in that when she uses the device, she can only access certain apps, books, and TV shows that you currently have on your device.

Kindle FreeTime Unlimited

Amazon has taken this feature a step further and offers an optional subscription plan to FreeTime users, which provides a curated selection of TV shows, apps, movies, and books specific for children ages 3 to 8 years old. This variety of media is continuously refreshed to keep children entertained with the newest apps, books, and videos.

This content will be available to only user profiles subscribed to FreeTime Unlimited. This available content will be in addition to any content already made permissible by the device owner.

Any content provided through FreeTime will not display ads, hyperlinks, social media, or options for purchasing items from within apps.

Normally, Kindle FreeTime Unlimited costs $4.99 per month, for one child. You can also choose an account for up to 6 children, which costs $9.99 per month. However, if you are an Amazon Prime subscriber, the fee is $2.99 for one child and $6.99 for up to six children.

Here are more details on the program:

http://www.amazon.com/gp/feature.html?docId=1000863021

Subscribe to Kindle FreeTime

Open the Kindle FreeTime app, either by finding and tapping the app icon from your Home screen or by visiting the parental controls screen within the settings screen (tap on the Kindle FreeTime app icon).

Tap on the Manage Content & Subscription button and enter in your parental control password. Then tap OK.

Second Screen

This new feature, becoming available November 2013, will be delivered to Kindle HD and Kindle HDX owners via a software update. In addition to owning one of these devices, other hardware requirements include a PlayStation 3, PlayStation 4, or 2013 Samsung Smart TV.

Second Screen allows users to play their Amazon purchased or rented video content on their TV or media streaming device. This enables users to turn the streaming device into the primary screen, freeing up the Kindle to do other tasks while watching the video on the TV/Streaming Device.

By using Second Screen, your HDX will become a remote control for playback control, X-Ray can be opened to give you more information about your show/movie, or check email and other tasks.

The Second Screen icon will appear on your device when you are viewing a video as long as you have an approved device listed above.

A Second Screen icon appears when you use the Instant Video application on your HDX. Just make sure that you have signed into your Instant Video application with your proper Amazon Account email and password.

Renting Textbooks

Amazon allows you to rent textbooks for a period of time (typically a minimum of 30 days and a maximum of 360) and save up to 80% off the list price. Sometimes, you also have the option to extend your rental 1 day at a time, as many times as you want if needed. Many textbooks, however, are only available for a specific period of time.

The best way to browse for Textbooks is not on your Kindle device, but on your computer. If you go to Amazon.com, you will see a "Shop by Department" icon in the upper left hand corner. Hover over this with your mouse, then scroll down and hover your mouse over "Books and Audio". On the right, under "Books" in orange, you should see "Textbooks" - click on this. You are now in the Kindle Textbooks store.

On the left hand side, you will see "Textbook Programs" in orange. Under this, click on "Textbook Rental". Now, you are in the "Textbook Rentals" page. You will see "Get Started – Rent Your Books Here:", with a search bar underneath. You can search for textbooks to rent by typing them in here.

Quick Tip: Many textbooks you search for will not be eligible for rental. It is helpful to type in "rental" after your search. (For example, search: "Biology rental"). Once you find a book you can rent, you will see a "Rent" option in the upper right hand corner, where your purchase options are located.

Click on the dot to the left of "Rent". Here you will see the rental details, including the Due Date. This book will ship to you physically, or via your Kindle if it is an eBook. Normally shipping will be free to return at the end of the rental term. You will notice the price is normally substantially reduced from the "Buy New" Price.

Immersion Reading

Immersion Reading allows you to listen to a professionally narrated Audible Audiobook and read the Kindle-edition at the same time. The program will highlight the text as it is read to you, so you can easily follow along. This is great for young children who are still learning how to read, foreigners who are trying to learn English, and anyone who is reading on-the-go.

To access Immersion Reading eligible content, tap Shop from the Content Library Menu, then tap "Books". Now, tap the 3 lined icon in the upper left hand corner to open the Navigation Panel.

Here, you will see a category title "Immersion Reading". Tapping this will bring you to all content that is Immersion-enabled. If you tap on a book, you will be taken to the description page. Underneath the book, you should see a note that says "Active Immersion Reading. Add professional narration for $___". Once you purchase the Kindle book, you will have the option to add professional narration that will highlight as it reads to you.

Accessories

Being as sleek and powerful as the Kindle Fire HDX is, you will want to ensure you do not damage the device or unnecessarily expose it to the elements. Amazon recommends a few different cases that will work well with your HDX.

Full Cases for Your HDX

Amazon Kindle Fire HDX Standing Polyurethane Origami Case (Kindle Fire HDX 7")

http://www.amazon.com/Amazon-Standing-Polyurethane-Origami-Mineral/dp/B00DR0B7Y8

This case will only fit a 7-inch HDX. This case is produced and sold by Amazon and it has a fairly innovative design. It claims to be the lightest and thinnest case for your HDX. The case attaches magnetically to your device, so there are no straps to fuss with, and the case integrates buttons so you have access to power and volume. The accessory has a soft inner lining and automatically wakes the device and puts it to sleep when you open and close the case's flap.

The beauty of the case is it folds out "origami-style" which means it can be propped up both vertically and horizontally for hands-free use.

Cons: There are a few downsides to the Origami-Case. First, there is no designated space for the speakers on the case, so if you plan on using the external speakers to listen to audio, you will need to remove from the case to get full quality sound.

Another downside is that the case leaves the corners of the device exposed, which means the HDX is still prone to some damage if it is dropped.

Lastly, the case has another relatively significant flaw that users commonly complain about: when the case is opened and the cover folded back (behind the device), the tablet sometimes shuts off. This may be due to the magnetic nature of the case.

That being said, the device has a ranking of around 4/5 stars, so overall most users are very happy with the case.

Belkin Chambray Cover (Kindle Fire HDX 7")

http://www.amazon.com/Belkin-Chambray-Cover-Kindle-Blacktop/dp/B00DQZOD8Q

Another option is the Belkin Chambray case, which is certified to use with the Kindle Fire HDX (note: it is only available for the 7-inch model). This main feature of this case is that it has an adjustable stand, which moves to allow you to position the device in different ways.

This means you can prop the case up steeply or flatter, depending on your position. The case comes in a number of colors and features a strap that wraps around your device securely.

Cons: One of the main downsides of the device is that it does not have a magnet to automatically wake or turn off the device when you open or close the case.

Another common complaint is that the cover of the case flops around (due to the flexibility for use as a stand) and does not fold back neatly, thus making the device difficult to use when you are holding the HDX (and don't have it propped up).

Otterbox Defender Standing Case (Kindle Fire HDX 7")

http://www.amazon.com/OtterBox-Defender-Standing-Kindle-Black/dp/B00DQZP7X6

By far the most durable and heavy-duty of the available cases is the Otterbox case. Otterbox is known for their smartphone and tablet cases, which are some of the best in the industry at protecting the devices. This case is certified to use with the Kindle Fire HDX 7-inch (will not fit the 8.9-inch). The case consists of a heavy plastic exterior that locks around the case - once the device is locked in, it will not come out due to normal usage. The cover closes shut over the screen, to keep your device completely sealed when not in use. It also comes with a screen protector, so the screen won't damage while it's in use. The case also has a stand, so you can prop it up to use when you are watching movies or viewing media. The device also has built-in buttons so you can access the power and volume controls.

Cons: The most obvious negative of the case is that it is relatively bulky. While the other cases are sleek and thin, this case is heavy and large, but provides your device with by far the most protection. While it won't protect it if it is submerged in water, it will protect it from any drops or there possible damages.

Sleeve Cases

Some other, more cost-effective options for protection are sleeve cases. These types of cases mainly consist of soft, flexible sleeves that you can slide your HDX into. They will not protect the device during use, as you will take the sleeve off to use. But they will protect it during transportation, ensuring the body or screen to not become scratched.

BUILT Neoprene Kindle Fire HDX 7" Slim Sleeve Case, Lush Flower (fits the all new Kindle Fire HD and HDX 7")

http://www.amazon.com/BUILT-Neoprene-Kindle-Sleeve-Flower/dp/B005I6DJF4

Built is a well-respected accessories company and produces cases for many popular devices. This case fits both the Kindle

Fire HD and HDX 7" (not the 8.9" HDX). This device is certified to use with your Kindle and features a soft inner lining and a form-fitting design, so your Kindle will fit snugly and not move around in the case. (You can even turn it upside down and your Kindle will stay put!).

Cons: This device is highly rated, and the only real con is that the designs are relatively feminine and seem to be catered to women. Also, the case doesn't protect the Kindle during use, which is inherent to all sleeve-style cases.

Amazon Kindle Fire HDX 7" Zip Sleeve, Charcoal (Kindle Fire HD and HDX 7")

http://www.amazon.com/Amazon-Kindle-Fire-Sleeve-Charcoal/dp/B005DOKM9M

Produced by Amazon, this case comes in a number of colors, is certified for Kindle use, and zips around the HDX to hold it safely. It is made of thin material and has a soft interior to keep your device safe and scratch free. Once zipped shut, there is no way for your Kindle to fall out of the case.

Cons: While this device is fairly highly rated, there are a few complaints among reviewers. First, is the case is said to comes with a "chemical/plastic" smell. Another complaint is that there is little padding on the interior (this contributes to it's slim profile) and overall the case is somewhat "barebones" for the price.

Miscellaneous Accessories

Marware Capacitive Stylus for Touchscreen Devices

You can use a stylus to navigate your HDX more precisely and also take advantage of drawing and learning applications. This stylus by Marware is highly rated, providing a smooth writing experience and an aluminum case for strong durability. This stylus can be used on any touchscreen device.

Cons: One of the main complaints of the stylus is that the clip (which you can use to attach to your case) comes apart after awhile. Also, the stylus features a rubber tip, which may not slide well on certain screens.

Before You Go...

Did you find this book helpful? Was it worth the few dollars?

Are you a master of your HDX yet? Or did this book confuse you?

Whether you found it to be extremely helpful, completely useless, or somewhere in between, your opinion is valued highly by us, the Amazon Marketplace, and most importantly – **fellow readers**.

With future updates provided to you for no additional cost, all feedback helps improve each new edition.

Please let us know what you thought and leave a review!

That will help inform future readers about what the book entails, and allows us to make critical adjustments in future editions – it only takes less than a minute.

Thank You,

Daniel Forrester

Made in the USA
San Bernardino, CA
15 January 2014